Claremont McKenna College

Claremont, California

Written by Hayes Humphreys

Layout and Edits by Jon Skindzier and Matt Hamman

Final Edits by Kelly Carey

*Additional contributions by Omid Gohari,
Joey Rahimi, and Luke Skurman*

ISBN # 1-4274-0279-5
© Copyright 2006 College Prowler
All Rights Reserved
Printed in the U.S.A.
www.collegeprowler.com

Last updated: 08/23/06

Special Thanks To: Babs Carryer, Andy Hannah, LaunchCyte, Tim O'Brien, Bob Sehlinger, Thomas Emerson, Dave Lehman, Daniel Fayock, Chris Babyak, The Donald H. Jones Center for Entrepreneurship, Terry Slease, Jerry McGinnis, Bill Ecenberger, Idie McGinty, Kyle Russell, Jacque Zaremba, Larry Winderbaum, Roland Allen, Jon Reider, Team Evankovich, Lauren Varacalli, Abu Noaman, Mark Exler, Daniel Steinmeyer, Jared Cohon, Gabriela Oates, David Koegler, Ditto Documents Services, Meryl Sustarsic, Jaime Myers, Adam Burns, Carrie Petersen, Jon Skindzier, Alyson Pope, Jesse Rapsack, Heather Estes, Christina Koshzow, Christopher Mason, Glen Meakem, and the Claremont McKenna College Bounce-Back Team.

College Prowler®
5001 Baum Blvd.
Suite 750
Pittsburgh, PA 15213

Phone: 1-800-290-2682
Fax: 1-800-772-4972
E-Mail: info@collegeprowler.com
Web Site: www.collegeprowler.com

How this all started...

When I was trying to find the perfect college, I used every resource that was available to me. I went online to visit school websites; I talked with my high school guidance counselor; I read book after book; I hired a private counselor. Sure, this was all very helpful, but nothing really told me what life was like at the schools I cared about. These sources weren't giving me enough information to be totally confident in my decision.

In all my research, there were only two ways to get the information I wanted.

The first was to physically visit the campuses and see if things were really how the brochures described them, but this was quite expensive and not always feasible. The second involved a missing ingredient: the students. Actually talking to a few students at those schools gave me a taste of the information that I needed so badly. The problem was that I wanted more but didn't have access to enough people.

In the end, I weighed my options and decided on a school that felt right and had a great academic reputation, but truth be told, the choice was still very much a crapshoot. I had done as much research as any other student, but was I 100 percent positive that I had picked the school of my dreams?

Absolutely not.

My dream in creating *College Prowler* was to build a resource that people can use with confidence. My own college search experience taught me the importance of gaining true insider insight; that's why the majority of this guide is composed of quotes from actual students. After all, shouldn't you hear about a school from the people who know it best?

I hope you enjoy reading this book as much as I've enjoyed putting it together. Tell me what you think when you get a chance. I'd love to hear your college selection stories.

Luke Skurman
CEO and Co-Founder
lukeskurman@collegeprowler.com

Welcome to College Prowler®

During the writing of College Prowler's guidebooks, we felt it was critical that our content was unbiased and unaffiliated with any college or university. We think it's important that our readers get honest information and a realistic impression of the student opinions on any campus—that's why if any aspect of a particular school is terrible, we (unlike a campus brochure) intend to publish it. While we do keep an eye out for the occasional extremist—the cheerleader or the cynic—we take pride in letting the students tell it like it is. We strive to create a book that's as representative as possible of each particular campus. Our books cover both the good and the bad, and whether the survey responses point to recurring trends or a variation in opinion, these sentiments are directly and proportionally expressed through our guides.

College Prowler guidebooks are in the hands of students throughout the entire process of their creation. Because you can't make student-written guides without the students, we have students at each campus who help write, randomly survey their peers, edit, layout, and perform accuracy checks on every book that we publish. From the very beginning, student writers gather the most up-to-date stats, facts, and inside information on their colleges. They fill each section with student quotes and summarize the findings in editorial reviews. In addition, each school receives a collection of letter grades (A through F) that reflect student opinion and help to represent contentment, prominence, or satisfaction for each of our 20 specific categories. Just as in grade school, the higher the mark the more content, more prominent, or more satisfied the students are with the particular category.

Once a book is written, additional students serve as editors and check for accuracy even more extensively. Our bounce-back team—a group of randomly selected students who have no involvement with the project—are asked to read over the material in order to help ensure that the book accurately expresses every aspect of the University and its students. This same process is applied to the 200-plus schools College Prowler currently covers. Each book is the result of endless student contributions, hundreds of pages of research and writing, and countless hours of hard work. All of this has led to the creation of a student information network that stretches across the nation to every school that we cover. It's no easy accomplishment, but it's the reason that our guides are such a great resource.

When reading our books and looking at our grades, keep in mind that every college is different and that the students who make up each school are not uniform—as a result, it is important to assess schools on a case-by-case basis. Because it's impossible to summarize an entire school with a single number or description, each book provides a dialogue, not a decision, that's made up of 20 different topics and hundreds of student quotes. In the end, we hope that this guide will serve as a valuable tool in your college selection process. Enjoy!

The College Prowler Team

CLAREMONT MCKENNA COLLEGE
Table of Contents

Introduction from the Author

CMC is not a typical small liberal arts school. Located in sunny Southern California, 35 miles east of Los Angeles, CMC is one of five undergraduate institutions joined together in the Claremont Consortium. All five campuses are connected, and in some ways it's kind of like a big university with different schools. Students can take classes at any of the campuses, join clubs, eat, and party across the borders. Sports and some academic programs are shared between the schools, but in other really important ways the schools are very distinct. The schools vary greatly in philosophy, atmosphere, and the makeup of the student bodies. Graduation requirements and core classes are different. Going to school at CMC is very different from going to school at Pomona, Mudd, Pitzer, or Scripps.

Academically, CMC is known for its economics and government programs, which deserve the attention. But thinking of CMC as an econ and gov school doesn't do justice to CMC's other strong departments. It is truly a liberal arts school with strong departments in everything from biology and chemistry to psychology, philosophy, and history. To graduate, everyone is required to take a class in almost every subject. Classes are small, usually capped at 19, and student participation is always a high priority, even in typically lecture-based classes. There are no teaching assistants, and professors are very available and interested in their students' well-being.

The student body is active, outgoing, and campus-centric. Most students live on campus to take part in the close-knit community atmosphere and lively social life. Because the weather is so nice, CMC life is outdoor-oriented, with lots of intramural sports, outdoor parties, and barbeques—no sunny afternoon is complete without a few bodies laying out in the sun.

The CMC student body is hugely diverse, especially in terms of interests, so almost anyone can be happy here. CMC supports an active intellectualism, meaning that while CMCers like to learn for the sake of learning, they know the classroom is only the first step in using ideas to shape the world. CMCers are involved in a ton of activities—and they have to be to make sure there's always a lot going on. Beyond these qualities though, CMCers come from all walks of life, and CMC's generous financial aid policy makes sure that price doesn't determine who comes to CMC—academic ability, extracurricular involvement, and personality do.

Hayes Humphreys, Author
Claremont McKenna College

By the Numbers

General Information

Claremont McKenna
890 Colombia Avenue
Claremont, CA 91711

Control:
Private

Academic Calendar:
Semesters

Religious Affiliation:
None

Founded:
1946

Web Site:
www.claremontmckenna.edu

Main Phone:
(909) 621-8000

Student Body

**Full-Time
Undergraduates:**
1,139

**Part-Time
Undergraduates:**
0

**Total Male
Undergraduates:**
616

**Total Female
Undergraduates:**
523

Admissions

Overall Acceptance Rate:
21%

Early Decision Acceptance Rate:
25%

Regular Acceptance Rate:
21%

Total Applicants:
3,734

Total Acceptances:
786

Freshman Enrollment:
271

Yield (% of admitted students who actually enroll):
34%

Early Decision Available?
Yes

Early Action Available?
No

Early Decision Deadline:
November 15

Early Decision Notification:
December 15

Regular Decision Deadline:
January 2

Regular Decision Notification:
April 1

Must-Reply-By Date:
May 1

Applicants Placed on Waiting List:
562

Applicants Accepting a Place on Waiting List:
197

Students Enrolled from Waiting List:
24

Transfer Applications Received:
194

Transfer Applications Accepted:
60

Transfer Students Enrolled:
38

Transfer Application Acceptance Rate:
30%

Common Application Accepted?
Yes

Supplemental Forms?
Yes, with an analytical essay

Admissions Phone:
(909) 621-8088

Admissions E-Mail:
admission@claremontmckenna.edu

Admissions Web Site:
www.claremontmckenna.edu/admission

SAT I or ACT Required?
Either

SAT I Range (25th–75th Percentile):
1310–1490

SAT I Verbal Range (25th–75th Percentile):
650–750

➡

→

**SAT I Math Range
(25th–75th Percentile):**
660–740

**ACT Composite Range
(25th–75th Percentile):**
29–33

**ACT English Range
(25th–75th Percentile):**
29–33

**ACT Math Range
(25th–75th Percentile):**
28–32

SAT II Requirements:
Recommended, but only
required if home-schooled

Freshman Retention Rate:
95%

**Top 10% of
High School Class:**
84%

Application Fee:
$50

**Students Also Applied to
These Schools:**
Georgetown University
Pomona College
Stanford University
UC Berkeley
UCLA

Financial Information

Full-Time Tuition:
$33,210

Room and Board:
$10,740

Books and Supplies:
$850

**Average Need-Based
Financial Aid Package
(including loans, work-study,
grants, and other sources):**
$25,674

**Students Who Applied
for Financial Aid:**
58%

Students Who Received Aid:
50%

Financial Aid Forms Deadline:
February 1

Financial Aid Phone:
(909) 621-8356

Financial Aid E-Mail:
finaid@claremontmckenna.edu

Financial Aid Web Site:
*www.claremontmckenna.
edu/finanaid*

Academics

The Lowdown On...
Academics

Degrees Awarded:
Bachelor

Most Popular Majors:
22% Economics
22% Political Science
15% Psychology
12% International Relations
11% History

Full-Time Faculty:
116

Faculty with Terminal Degree:
96%

→

Student-to-Faculty Ratio:
9:1

Average Course Load:
4 courses

Class Sizes:
Fewer than 20 Students: 82%
20 to 49 Students: 17%
50 or More Students: 1%

Graduation Rates:
Four-Year: 82%
Five-Year: 87%
Six-Year: 88%

Special Degree Options

Accelerated MA in economics, accelerated MA in political science, accelerated MA in psychology, BA/BS in economics and engineering (3+2), BA/BS in management engineering (3+2), BA/MS in applied biology (3+2), JD from Columbia University through the Accelerated Interdisciplinary Legal Education Program (3+3), Robert A. Day 4+1 BA/MBA Program

AP Test Score Requirements

Possible credit or placement for scores of 4 or 5

IB Test Score Requirements

Possible credit or placement for scores of 6 or 7

Best Places to Study

Outside in the sunshine, reading rooms, lounges, the library, computer labs

Sample Academic Clubs

Claremont Historical Society, Passwords, Pre-Law Society

Did You Know?

 Claremont students can **cross-register for any classes across the Consortium**, often including graduate-level classes, and students can even major through another college while still receiving a Claremont McKenna College degree.

Claremont McKenna does not offer minors. Instead, students may choose to dual major, which slightly reduces the course load of both majors, making two areas of study more manageable. Best of all, tell someone at home you're a bio-lit dual major, and they'll assume you're actually doing the full double!

Claremont also offers sequences, which allow students to **get credit for other areas of study**. Some examples are the Leadership, Gender Studies, Human Rights, Genocide and Holocaust Studies and Financial Economics sequences. Students may only get credit for one sequence.

Students Speak Out On...
Academics

> "I admire and respect my professors a great deal, yet I feel completely comfortable talking to them about current events, career advice, and anything else that crosses my mind."

Q "To a science student, **Claremont seems to be full of government, international relations, and econ people**, so people who aren't one of those feel like they should take at least a few government or econ classes, because that's what the school seems to be known for."

Q "It's a **great academic atmosphere** without the cutthroat competitiveness of an East Coast school."

Q "CMC is known for their combination of practicality with a liberal arts education. It emphasizes business, especially work in investment banking, consulting, and accounting. The workload can be insane. Of course, those who do not want to work can do a less intensive major and take easy courses. But for the most part, **you won't get out of this college without some dedication** (especially after freshman year, it's much harder). The professors are generally amazing people. Of course, we have quirky professors (like every other school), but the difference between CMC and most schools is that we actually get to know our professors. We go to lunch with them, we see them at the Athenaeum, they are in our PE classes (yoga, at least), and we see them around campus and town all the time."

Q "**The workload is what you make of it**. If you take easier courses and put forth little effort, you can get by with a very small amount of work. However, if you have a more involved major, you will need to put in more of your time, and not just for paper writing or studying, but for meetings with groups or professors outside of class."

Q "CMC's workload is great in that **you can directly influence the amount of work** depending on what you want out of college."

Q "Professors are **very helpful and friendly**. Their lectures are engaging and interesting."

Q "It's a friendly kind of competitiveness in terms of academics. I have heard horror stories from Ivy League schools of students sabotaging other students' projects and such, something that would never in a million years happen here. **Healthy competition that makes everyone better** and smarter is how we operate."

Q "There are **lots of government and economics majors**, but there are tons of people who are just majoring in whatever they want, getting some real-world experience through internships, and still have no idea what they want to do with their lives (I am one of those)."

Q "What's great about having more of a balance of views is that it leads to some **awesome debates in and out of class**, and you tend to learn more if you don't hear the same point of view all the time."

Q "**The workload is perfect for me**; I feel like I worked so hard to get into CMC, and I'm paying so much money that if I wasn't getting everything out of my academic experience here, it'd be a waste."

Q "Professors are **very demanding and they expect a lot**, but they're not unreasonable in the amount of work they assign or in their grading methods."

Q "Claremont is **world-renowned** for economics and government, and our PPE (Philosophy, Politics, and Economics) major is also quite well regarded."

Q "**You'll have a lot of homework** and you'll work really hard, but at the end of the semester, you'll feel so great that you learned so much, and the good grade you earned will mean so much more."

Q "Most professors seem **genuinely interested in whether students learn**, and they're more than happy to meet with students to go over difficult material."

The College Prowler Take On...
Academics

Professors at Claremont McKenna are friendly, hands-on teachers who care about the academic and general well-being of their students. With most classes enrolling fewer than 19 students, it's easy to be heard in class; even in lecture classes, discussions are encouraged. While there is a hefty workload, Claremont is not a grind school, and generally, the work ebbs and flows in regular cycles. It is not unusual to have two weeks of intense paper-writing and midterm-taking followed by a few weeks of reading. It is essential to have prioritizing skills at Claremont, since keeping up on homework, extracurriculars, and social life is a constant—but manageable—juggling act. Most classes are structured around three or four major assignments; because there are so few, professors expect a high level of effort and a certain amount of creativity and originality. Students are supportive of one another, no one judges anyone else by the grades they get, and most classes assign group work.

Government and economics are the two most popular majors at the school, but that shouldn't deter anyone not considering either, as many of the other departments are diamonds in the rough. How does taking your introductory psychology class with Diane Halpern, the president of the American Psychological Association, sound? Students tend to take classes from every professor in the department, and the resources of the whole group will be available when looking for jobs, internships, or research opportunities.

The College Prowler® Grade on

Academics: A

A high Academics grade generally indicates that professors are knowledgeable, accessible, and genuinely interested in their students' welfare. Other determining factors include class size, how well professors communicate, and whether or not classes are engaging.

Local Atmosphere

The Lowdown On...
Local Atmosphere

Region:
Southern California

City, State:
Claremont, CA

Setting:
Suburban

**Distance from
Pasadena:**
30 minutes

Distance from LA:
45 minutes

**Distance from
the Beach:**
1 hour

Points of Interest:
Disneyland
The Getty Museum
Hollywood
Santa Monica Pier
Universal Studios
Venice Beach

➜

Shopping Malls:

Montclair Plaza
www.montclairplaza.com

Ontario Mills
www.ontariomills.com

Victoria Gardens
www.victoriagardensie.com

Major Sports Teams:

Anaheim Angels (baseball)

Anaheim Mighty Ducks
(hockey)

Los Angeles Clippers
(basketball)

Los Angeles Dodgers
(baseball)

Los Angeles Galaxy (soccer)

Los Angeles Lakers (basketball)

Sacramento Kings (basketball)

San Diego Chargers (football)

Movie Theaters:

Edwards La Verne

1950 Foothill Boulevard
La Verne, CA 91750

(909) 392-4894

AMC Ontario Mills 30

4549 Mills Circle
Ontario, CA 91764

(909) 484-3000

City Web Site

www.ci.claremont.ca.us

Did You Know?

5 Fun Facts about Claremont:

- **The Rancho Cucamonga Quakes**, an Angels minor league baseball club in the area, has dollar beer nights. Throw a couple back, and you won't even wonder why a dinosaur is their mascot.

- **Ben Harper's family** owns the folk music store in the Village.

- Claremont McKenna sits in the shadow of the **tallest mountain in Southern California**, so in the spring, you can hit the beach and the ski slopes in the same day!

- The **tallest buildings in Claremont** are the seven story South Quad towers on campus.

- There is a **new extension to the Village being** built with a movie theater, restaurants, and more student-oriented stores.

Famous People from Claremont:

Kylie Bivens, Ben Harper

Local Slang:

The Village – The small collection of shops and restaurants near campus.

Students Speak Out On...
Local Atmosphere

"Everything you need is on campus; LA is near enough to go, but there really is no need. The atmosphere in the Village is really chill, but otherwise, it's useless."

Q "The other four schools surrounding CMC's campus create a lively environment filled with students and bustling with activities that many other small liberal arts colleges lack. Instead of feeling like I go to a small, isolated school, **Claremont McKenna feels more like a mid-sized university** (but with all the benefits of a small school). Plus, our biggest sports rivals are only a block away! How convenient is that?"

Q "Claremont the town is full of **old, rich, white people**, but overall, it's a nice little bubble to live in protected from San Bernardino county to the east, and crappy LA everywhere else."

Q "The Claremont Village is small but has a **very pleasant atmosphere**. There are a number of restaurants and a few good ice cream places. The stores in the Village are catered more to an older, wealthier crowd, rather than college students. However, as you stray out of the city of Claremont and drive along Foothill, there are plenty of other options."

Q "**The Village sucks**, although the Press is always good for a drunken brawl and pitchers of Heffewizen. Go to LA—it's worth the drive."

Q "There are fun things to do, but since **there is usually so much happening on campus**, most people stick around. If you get sick of CMC or feel like you aren't seeing new faces, just take a few steps in any direction, and instantly, you are someplace new."

Q "The atmosphere in the Village is awesomely unique. The **restaurants and stores are all one-of-a-kind**. Plus, everything is in walking distance. There really isn't anything that I would say to stay away from, but definitely check out the hole-in-the-wall Mexican restaurants around the area. As for things to do, getting around LA is tough if you don't have a car, but if you do, there are a million outside things to do. If not, being on campus is just as entertaining."

Q "**The Village has its own unique charm**. There are a number of excellent restaurants for students to take advantage of, ranging from traditional Italian to delicious sushi to a Spanish tapas bar. There are also more casual places for relaxing, like the numerous coffee and smoothie shops, sandwich places, and quaint stores for students to explore."

Q "The Village has a **sleepy, small-town sort of feel**. Its ivy-covered buildings, brick architecture, and tree-lined streets make it a nice place just to stroll around. It is a great place to go for dinner or coffee with friends. But if you are looking for the typical college town, Claremont is not it. There isn't really a bar or clubbing scene in the immediate area. If you have a car on campus, LA is awesome. But CMC hosts so many parties and provides so many activities on campus, most students aren't really looking to spend a lot of time off campus until senior year."

The College Prowler Take On...
Local Atmosphere

Going to college in Southern California means that it is a drive to get just about everywhere. The only sign of life within walking distance is the Village, a small town most often described as "sleepy." While not far off the mark, this description is slightly unfair. The Village is home to quite a few good, moderately pricey restaurants. The Press is a popular bar, but wild and crazy aren't exactly the right words for it.

Claremont McKenna sits on one of the main thoroughfares of the Inland Empire, however, so there are many college-student-friendly establishments within an easy drive. There are bars galore, movie theaters, malls, major grocery stores, an awesome bowling alley (dollar beer nights are a must), and more Targets, Best Buys and Wal-Marts than you can shake a stick at (that's a lot). Further afield is Disneyland, Six Flags, Joshua Tree National Park, Las Vegas, and of course, Los Angeles. Claremont students don't head into LA every weekend, but when they do make the hour-long trip, it's often to go to the beach, be on *The Price Is Right*, visit the Getty Center and other art museums, see traveling Broadway shows, or go clubbing. Las Vegas is a really popular weekend option for those over 21. Other CMCers spend the occasional weekend in Palm Springs or San Diego, both about an hour and a half away. For all the skiers and boarders, Big Bear Mountain is an hour drive. Claremont isn't a suitcase campus by any stretch of the imagination, but its surroundings do provide nice diversions from time to time.

The College Prowler® Grade on

Local Atmosphere: B

A high Local Atmosphere grade indicates that the area surrounding campus is safe and scenic. Other factors include nearby attractions, proximity to other schools, and the town's attitude toward students.

Safety & Security

The Lowdown On...
Safety & Security

Number of CMC Security Officers:

14 full-time uniformed Campus Safety officers, 6 dispatchers, 25–40 reserve officers

CMC Campus Security Phone:

(909) 607-8000

Safety Services:

Call-boxes

Student escort service

Self-defense PE classes

Sexual assault awareness and protection workshop

→

Health Services:
Blood tests
Counseling services
Eating disorder awareness
Flu shots
General check-ups
Immunizations
Vision tests
Women's health services
X-rays

Health Center:
Health Education Outreach
757 College Way
(909) 607-3602
Monday–Tuesday, Thursday–Friday 8:30 a.m.–5 p.m., Wednesday 8:30 a.m.–7 p.m.

Did You Know?

HEO provides all kinds of **free goodies for safer sex**. For those not interested, or otherwise unsuccessful in love, they provide workshops in self pleasure.

Dorms can schedule a **lounge massage lesson** for stress relief!

Generally, **city police are not allowed on campus** unless invited by Camp Sec, so get friendly with your local officers if you anticipate any 'incidents.'

Students Speak Out On...
Safety & Security

"I feel extremely safe around the five colleges, particularly at CMC. There are almost always people around, and you constantly see security guards perusing the campuses in golf carts."

Q "I come from Sioux Falls, SD, and I believe the surrounding area feels just as **safe and secure**."

Q "I hear about stuff occasionally going on around the campus, but **I have never witnessed, experienced, or known anyone who has had anything happen** to them. No school is 100 percent safe, because they are all publicly accessible, but CMC is definitely up there."

Q "Most **people leave their doors unlocked**, although since that is the case, stuff does get stolen from time to time. In general, it's very safe, though. We are kind of in the middle of suburbia, so the biggest threat is basically an angry soccer mom or something."

Q "It's so safe, it's bad, because **it leads people not to lock their doors**. The only problems are when the punk Claremont High School kids come on campus trying to sneak into parties and end up stealing stuff or starting fights."

Q "Camp Sec is usually good at letting kids have their fun and stepping in when things get out of hand. **Some of them do have power trips, though**."

Q "**Security does a great job**, but what really makes the campus safe is the fact that it is so small. You are seldom in a situation where there isn't someone around you know."

Q "Safety has been an issue recently. The difference between my freshman and sophomore years appears to be dramatic. **More car break-ins, some assaults** off of 6th Street, more theft (in south quad, at least). It's still much safer than many other campuses, though."

Q "For a small girl, **it is scary at night** on 6th street. Always have a guy walk you."

Q "I'm a pretty paranoid person, but **I've never once felt unsafe** on campus."

Q "**CMC offers far more security** than is probably necessary for the safe bubble of Claremont."

The College Prowler Take On...
Safety & Security

Claremont McKenna is so safe that students like to joke about the "CMC Bubble" that shields them from the real world. This is partly because Claremont has found an ideal balance with the consortium security, so Campus Security (Camp Sec) is always there when students want them and rarely there when students don't. Although there are security phones all over campus and a student escort service, you'd be hard-pressed to find a student who's used either. Dorms require ID cards to enter at all times, and any buildings open past 10 also require an ID swipe to get in. In the dorms, most students live with their doors unlocked and open to make it easier for friends to come visit. There is the occasional laptop or bike theft, but even those are rare, while serious crimes are almost nonexistent.

Claremont students don't find themselves walking to very many places off campus, other than the Village, and that walk is mostly through other safe college campuses. Students are in their cars to go anywhere else, which means that kids aren't getting mugged on the street. Off-campus parties are rare, but when they do happen, the student government often provides a bus, or kids drive themselves. As a group, CMCers take drunk driving seriously (there's no faster way to end a fun night), and are good about choosing designated drivers. There are a few nastier-looking areas a bit south of Claremont McKenna, but there is no reason to go there at night, and they are totally safe during the day.

A-

The College Prowler® Grade on
Safety & Security:
A-

A high grade in Safety & Security means that students generally feel safe, campus police are visible, blue-light phones and escort services are readily available, and safety precautions are not overly necessary.

Computers

The Lowdown On...
Computers

High-Speed Network?
Yes

Number of Computers:
220

Number of Labs:
3

Wireless Network?
Yes

Operating Systems:
Mac OS X, Windows

24-Hour Labs:
Poppa Lab in Adams Hall and
South Park in Stark Hall

Discounted Software

Some Macintosh software is discounted at the Apple Store in the Huntley Bookstore.

Free Software

Norton AntiVirus

Charge to Print?

None

Did You Know?

Technician jobs are some of the highest-paying on campus, and only require a basic understanding of computers.

Students Speak Out On...
Computers

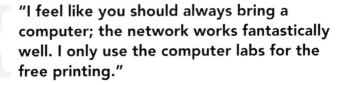

"I feel like you should always bring a computer; the network works fantastically well. I only use the computer labs for the free printing."

Q "We used to say that CMC was so wired that you could access the Internet from everywhere but the bathrooms. However, **we have recently gone wireless**, meaning the bathrooms are no longer off-limits, and honestly, student productivity is up 42 percent."

Q "I like that **we have a great technology assistance staff**, because I'm a little computer illiterate. Between LTAs and RTAs, there is a lot of tech support provided if you need it. My RTA even helped me connect my Xbox to the network."

Q "We have an incredible staff of both professionals and students who make computer issues on campus much easier to deal with. There is one student from every dorm hired to be on-call basically 24/7 in case you have a computer crash at 3 a.m. the night before a paper is due. **It's easy to get help**."

Q "Bringing your own computer is recommended, because students frequently need to write papers, receive e-mails, and of course, communicate via Instant Messenger. The **computer labs at CMC are easily accessible**, staffed with students nearly 24 hours, and usually have plenty of free computers. CMC also offers its students free printing, so leave your printers at home!"

Q "**The labs can get very crowded**. A personal computer is almost necessary, but you can survive without one. Resident Technology Assistants (RTAs) are readily available if you need help with your computer, which is extremely comforting for non-computer people like me."

Q "The computer network is very fast, and it does not restrict you from anything. **I would suggest bringing your own computer**, but it is definitely not needed because of the on-campus labs."

Q "Computer labs are good and empty, except around thesis time when it gets ridiculous (and they overheat Poppa, which makes you sleepy). The network is fast and great, and you should definitely bring your own computer because it's just so convenient. I think **I only know one person without a computer, and he's in hell**."

Q "**Bring your own computer**, but you don't need a laptop in class. Of course, you'll never get any work done in your room, so expect to spend a lot of time in the labs, which do get crowded in the evenings."

Q "I know nothing about computers, but **I've never had any problems with the network**. The computer labs can definitely get crowded around crunch time, and if possible, you should definitely have your own computer. A laptop is ideal so you can take advantage of the wireless Internet."

Q "Very few students are without access to their own computers, and as such, the computer labs are most often used for printing of assignments or for a place to escape to do work outside the distractions of one's own dorm room. **There is generally space at the labs**, but space can be limited at certain times, such as the period right before a popular class time, or before the senior thesis date when seniors escape to the labs to work."

Q "**CMC is wireless** now. Yay!"

Q "Recently, because of a switch to more efficient servers, the network has been down a lot more. However, in the past, it has run very smoothly. Computer labs are generally crowded when thesis deadline comes around. Other than that, I rarely have problems getting a computer. Bringing **your own computer is a must**. A laptop with wireless is so hassle-free."

The College Prowler Take On...
Computers

Technology is highly valued at Claremont McKenna, and the school tries to keep up with the pace of development. Even so, computing is easy for even the most computer-illiterate at Claremont. In 2005 the school went wireless, which allows every student to have the stereotypical experience of paper-writing out in the inspiring California sunshine. Whether plugged in or not, Internet at Claremont is as fast as it gets. Most students bring their own computers, but the school provides three computer labs on campus, two of which are open 24 hours a day. Finding a computer isn't usually an issue, but in the weeks before senior theses are due, the labs do get cramped. The computers in the labs are easy to use and are updated frequently. The school provides all the software needed for classes.

Claremont makes using computers as simple as possible. Resident Technology Assistants (RTAs) live in each dorm and are available during all waking hours to solve everything from computer emergencies to virus protection to software issues. The labs are staffed well into the night to help anyone with computer issues there. Printing is free and unlimited, and every student gets a gigabyte on the central server to store files that they wish to access all over campus and protect from local computer failure. File sharing is common, both over the internal network and with programs like KaZaa and Limewire. Bottom line: CMCers are technologically spoiled!

The College Prowler® Grade on
Computers: A

A high grade in Computers designates that computer labs are available, the computer network is easily accessible, and the campus's computing technology is up-to-date.

Facilities

The Lowdown On...
Facilities

Student Center:
Emett Student Center

Athletic Centers:
Ducey Gymnasium
Frank G. Wells Fitness Center
R. Ernest Smith Weight Room

Campus Size:
42 acres

Libraries:
4

Popular Places to Chill:
Afternoon Tea in the Athenaeum

The Coop at Pomona

The Hub in the Student Center

The Motley at Scripps

Outside (get a tan; white is outlawed in California)

Snack Time in Collins

What Is There to Do on Campus?

Grab a bite at the Hub, have dinner at the Athenaeum, play basketball on the dunk hoops, volleyball on one of the many courts around campus, play bocce, play pool in the Student Center, pond" your friends on their birthdays, see a movie in Pickford or in Pomona's Smith Campus Center, tan by the pool, or use the rock-climbing wall in Ducey.

Movie Theater on Campus?

No, but movies are often screened in Pickford Auditorium.

Bar on Campus?

No

Coffeehouse on Campus?

Yes, the Motley on Scripps's campus

Favorite Things to Do on Campus

Afternoon Tea: Rice Krispie treats the size of your head, and if you're there in time, mammoth chocolate-covered strawberries

Snack in Collins Dining Hall at night: Drop the books, run to Collins, see some friends, get a cup full of soft-serve, grab a chicken nugget or two and some breakfast for the morning.

Campus Sports: Campus golf of all varieties (normal, disc or monster golf), or a lazy Saturday afternoon game of bocce

Students Speak Out On...
Facilities

"The student facilities on campus are very user-friendly. You basically don't have to wait to use them, and can use them for as long as you'd like."

Q "**In a word: utilitarian**. Everything works, it's user friendly, but if there was a pretty way to build it, we didn't do it."

Q "The library is pretty good. If there is a book that our library doesn't have, we can easily get it from another academic SoCal library for free. Athletics are generally good. We have **nice facilities for teams**, but the gym with exercise machines is a little lacking, I think. The student center is a little dead. It was poorly planned to be in two parts and not in the center of campus, making it not the primary place to hang out. The dorm lounges vary a lot in how nice they are."

Q "The facilities of CMC are fantastic, clean, and aesthetically pleasing. The Hub and Student Center lack personality, in comparison to places like the Motley at Scripps and the Grove House at Pitzer. **The library is quite dingy**, and not a very comfortable place to spend long periods of time."

Q "Even your very own dorm room is kept clean by the **weekly cleaning service**."

Q "**Everything's super nice**—we're trying to build a new gym, but we keep running out of money. The library is fantastic, and we don't really have a student center, but it's okay for what it is."

Q "**The weight room is horrible** and in desperate need of repair, however the athletic department won't budge— they didn't replace any dumbbells until one broke, and even then, they only replaced a few."

Q "We are **not the prettiest college** (I say, Scripps and Pomona are). Our gym, however, is awesome."

Q "The student center is pretty lacking, but to be honest, with a small school, it's tough to really do too much. Plus, there are other student centers on the 5Cs that are usable, too. **The library is awesome**, though."

Q "**Most of the facilities are excellent**, with the exception of the gym and workout facilities. However, those facilities are being expanded and updated in the next few years. The library has an amazing collection and very helpful staff."

The College Prowler Take On...
Facilities

Claremont McKenna's campus is well groomed and maintained, almost to the point of obsessive compulsiveness. The grass is mowed religiously, the planters are replanted seemingly every month, and building interiors are spotless every morning. The oldest buildings on campus are only 60 years old. Mostly beige, utilitarian structures with red Spanish tile roofs, the buildings aren't spectacular, but they aren't eyesores either. There is a very cool new dorm in the final planning stages, so students who end up on the south side of campus can expect some noise through 2008. The Five College Consortium shares many facilities, which means more for all. The library is huge, there are six dining halls available, four cafés, a coffeehouse, three fitness centers, and an impressive theater complex. Claremont's workout facility is full of modern machinery donated by an alumnus who founded the LifeFitness Corporation. The Emett Student Center houses pool tables, a café called the Hub, satellite TVs, and the student store.

While it's easy to stay on campus for entertainment needs, students will have to tap the surrounding area for most other basic needs like groceries and restaurants. The student government does provide a shuttle to Target and Best Buy on some weekends, but generally, students are responsible for their own transport, and most students don't find getting the things they need off campus particularly inconvenient.

B

The College Prowler® Grade on

A high Facilities grade indicates that the campus is aesthetically pleasing and well-maintained; facilities are state-of-the-art, and libraries are exceptional. Other determining factors include the quality of both athletic and student centers and an abundance of things to do on campus.

Campus Dining

The Lowdown On...
Campus Dining

Freshman Meal Plan Requirement?

All students living in dorms must be on a meal plan.

Meal Plan Average Cost:

16 meals per week – $5,110 per year

12 meals per week – $4,700 per year

8 meals per week – $4,380 per year

Places to Grab a Bite with Your Meal Plan:

Collins Dining Hall

Food: Grille, vegetables, vegan, pizza, deli

Location: Claremont McKenna

Hours: Monday–Friday
7:30 a.m.–9:30 a.m.,
11 a.m.–1 p.m., 5 p.m.–7 p.m.,
Saturday–Sunday
10:30 a.m.–12:30 p.m.,
4:45 p.m.–6:15 p.m.

→

The Coop

Food: Burgers, salads, smoothies, shakes

Location: Smith Campus Center, Pomona

Hours: Monday–Thursday 9 a.m.–12 a.m., Friday 9 a.m.–1:30 a.m., Saturday–Sunday 12 p.m.–1:30 a.m.

Frary Dining Hall

Food: Cafeteria-style

Location: Pomona North Campus

Hours: Monday–Friday 7:30 a.m.–10 a.m., 11:30 a.m.–1 p.m., 5 p.m.–8 p.m., Saturday–Sunday 9 a.m.–11 a.m., 11 a.m.–1 p.m., 5:30 p.m.–7 p.m.

Frank Dining Hall

Food: Cafeteria-style

Location: Pomona South Campus

Hours: Monday–Friday 7:30 a.m.–10 a.m., 11:30 a.m.–1 p.m., 5 p.m.–7 p.m., Saturday–Sunday 11 a.m.–1 p.m., 5:30 p.m.–7 p.m.

The Grove House

Food: Lunch selections

Location: Pitzer

Hours: Monday–Thursday 9 a.m.–4 p.m., 7 p.m.–11 p.m., Friday 9 a.m.–4 p.m., Saturday 9 a.m.–4 p.m., 12 p.m.–3 p.m., Sunday 7 p.m.–11 p.m.

Hoch-Shanahan Dining Commons

Food: Pizza, rotisserie oven, sushi, ethnic, deli

Location: Harvey Mudd

Hours: Monday–Friday 7:30 a.m.–9:30 a.m., 11:15 a.m.–1 p.m., 5 p.m.–7 p.m., Saturday–Sunday 10:30 a.m.–12:45 p.m.

The Hub

Food: Salads, sandwiches, snack foods

Location: Emett Student Center, Claremont McKenna

Hours: Monday–Wednesday 11 a.m.–11 p.m., Thursday–Friday 11 a.m.–12 a.m., Saturday 12 p.m.–4:30 p.m.

Jay's Place

Food: Pizza, sandwiches, snacks

Location: Platt Campus Center, Harvey Mudd

Hours: Sunday–Thursday 7 p.m.–1 a.m., Friday–Saturday 7 p.m.–2 a.m.

Malott Commons

Food: Cafeteria-style

Location: Scripps Campus

Hours: Monday–Friday 7:30 a.m.–10 a.m., 11:15 a.m.–1:15 p.m., 5 p.m.–7 p.m., Saturday–Sunday 10:30 a.m.–12:30 p.m., 5 p.m.–6:30 p.m.

The Mandarin Café

Food: Asian Pacific

Location: Gold Campus Center, Pitzer

Hours: Hours vary, as the Café is student-operated, but it's generally open 10 a.m–8 p.m.

McConnell Bistro

Food: Cafeteria-style

Location: Pitzer

Hours: 7:30 a.m.–10 a.m., 11:15 a.m.–1:30 p.m., 5 p.m.–7 p.m., Saturday–Sunday 10:30 a.m.–12:30 p.m., 5 p.m.–6:30 p.m.

The Motley Coffeehouse

Food: Coffee, pastries

Location: Scripps

Hours: Sunday–Thursday 8 a.m.–12 a.m., Friday 8 a.m.–5 p.m., Saturday 12 p.m.–5 p.m.

Oldenborg Dining Hall

Food: Cafeteria-style

Location: Pomona North Campus

Hours: Monday–Friday 11:45 a.m.–12:45 p.m.

Sagehen Café

Food: Upscale restaurant-style; wraps, pasta, seafood

Location: Smith Campus Center, Pomona

Hours: Monday–Wednesday 11 a.m.–2 p.m., 5 p.m.–9 p.m., Thursday–Saturday 5 p.m.–9 p.m.

Off-Campus Places to Use Your Meal Plan:

Your meal plan is useable at all of the dining options throughout the Five College Consortium.

Student Favorites:

The Coop

The Motley

24-Hour Dining:

None

Did You Know?

On very special, very wonderful nights, **the In-N-Out truck** will visit campus.

Students Speak Out On...
Campus Dining

"The dining halls are great, particularly because you have a number of options. Scripps is probably my personal favorite, because they have a lot of healthy options, but it depends on what you like."

Q "Compared to other schools' foods that I have tasted, **we have it great**—we also have six dining halls to choose from, so it easy to shake things up."

Q "The food is probably **some of the best food you will get at college**. I mean, it's still college food, so it isn't five-star dining, and you will get sick of it towards the end of semester, but you'll be able to hack it here a lot longer than most other places. CMC, Pomona, and Scripps dining halls are all good; Harvey Mudd has steak nights on Sunday nights; Pitzer is horrible for anything except sandwich bar at lunch."

Q "One of the nicest things about the 5Cs is the ability to **eat at a different dining hall almost every night** of the week."

Q "CMC's dining hall offers the **most extensive salad and fresh fruit bar of any of the colleges**, fresh made smoothies and omelets at breakfast, an Italian or Chinese wok option at every dinner, and numerous other hot and cold food choices. Sunday through Thursday the dining hall reopens at 10:30 p.m. for snack, a free meal prepared by the College to cure the late-night cravings of hard-working students."

Q "**I love the food**. Good variety, six main dining halls in total, and lots of opportunities to make stuff yourself if you don't like it. There is also one restaurant on each campus, making basically four greasy spoons and one excellent coffeehouse (the Motley at Scripps). The three best dining halls are Collins (CMC), Frary (Pomona), and Scripps. The quality of the cafeteria food is pretty good, considering it's dining hall food."

Q "Collins is great until you get used to it around sophomore year, but you can always change things up by going to the other campuses' dining halls and getting something new. The Hub's okay, I like the Coop at Pomona a lot better, and **the Motley is good for coffee** unless you mind all the hippie free trade stuff."

Q "The food is some of the **best in the country**."

Q "Food on campus is terrible. I scoped out the local dining scene, and I **prefer to eat off campus** instead."

Q "CMC is good for **vegan options**."

Q "Collins has a **good selection of prepared dishes**, but also has a pretty good salad and sandwich bar, so you can put together things on your own. Scripps' dining hall, Malott Commons has great chicken and serves sushi on Fridays. Pomona's North Campus dining hall, Frary, has really good pizza and an ever popular burrito/taco night. Harvey Mudd recently rebuilt their dining hall, the décor is really nice, and I think it has the best salad bar."

Q "What I like best about the food on campus is that CMC **students may dine at any of the dining halls of the Claremont Colleges campuses**. Thus, there are six dining halls open to students for meals (seven at lunchtime, when Pomona's language residence hall has a cafeteria open). Additionally, there are on-campus locations where students can use flex dollars from the meal plan. My favorite of these places is the Motley, a coffeehouse on Scripps's campus."

Q "Collins has a great brunch, **Scripps usually has a good dinner** (especially on sushi night, Friday night). With the opening of Mudd's new dining hall, steak night has been much improved (in fact, every night has been). Frary is also good for dinner and breakfast (the egg white omelettes are the best at Frary; Collins is improving). Frary also has smoothies for breakfast (except during the weekends, I think), which is fabulous."

The College Prowler Take On...
Campus Dining

Claremont McKenna students are spoiled not only by having one good dining on campus, but also by the availability of five other dining halls within a five minute walk. Collins Dining Hall is in a central location on campus and is where Claremont students eat most of their meals. It's definitely a cafeteria, but the food is pretty high-quality. There is also a ton of variety with a big salad bar, a grill, vegan/vegetarian bar, sandwich bar, and a wok station where a chef stir-fries made-to-order dishes. With custom-made smoothies and omelets, weekend brunch is delicious as well. As an added bonus, the dining hall reopens at 10:30 p.m. during the week for a late-night snack.

Students also frequently opt to eat at the Athenaeum, an impressively classy dining room that hosts nightly dinner speaking events. The food at the Ath is a big step above the rest; the dessert chef also does his part, providing succulent pies, tarts, and cakes. The main attraction to the Ath is the speakers, of course, but the chance to eat a great meal while listening to the likes of Salman Rushdie, Newt Gingrich, Janet Reno, Spike Lee, and Archbishop Desmond Tutu is a welcome bonus. The Claremont meal plan also gives students access to the five other dining halls in the consortium. Everyone quickly learns to catch the best of all the campus eateries, like Pitzer lunch, sushi night at Scripps, steak night at Harvey Mudd, and Little Italy day at Claremont. Dining halls are all-you-can-eat, but for mid-meal snacks there are cafés or coffee shops on all of the campuses.

The College Prowler® Grade on

Campus Dining: A

The grade on Campus Dining addresses the quality of both school-owned dining halls and independent on-campus restaurants as well as the price, availability, and variety of food.

Off-Campus Dining

The Lowdown On...
Off-Campus Dining

Restaurant Prowler:
Popular Places to Eat!

21 Choices Frozen Yogurt
Food: Ice cream
817 Foothill Blvd.
(909) 621-7175
www.21choices.com
Cool Features: Cold stone-style frozen yogurt with mix-ins
Price: $4–$6
Hours: Daily 11 a.m.–11 p.m.

42nd St. Bagel
Food: Bagels, breakfast food
225 Yale Ave.
(909) 624-7655
Price: $5–$8
Hours: Monday–Friday 6 a.m.–6 p.m., Saturday–Sunday 6:30 a.m.–5 p.m.

Aladdin Jr.
Food: Middle Eastern
3161 N. Garey Ave.
(909) 593-3887
Cool Features: Hookah bar, amazing hummus, kebabs and shawarma

→

(Aladdin Jr., continued)

Price: $15 hookah, $10 main dishes, $5 gyros

Hours: Daily 11 a.m.–2 a.m.

Aruffo's

Food: Italian

126 Yale Ave.

(909) 624-9624

Cool Features: Good date place, excellent pasta.

Price: $20–$25

Hours: Sunday–Thursday 11 a.m.–8:30 p.m. Friday–Saturday 11 a.m.–9:30 p.m.

BC Café

Food: Breakfast

701 Indian Hill Blvd.

(909) 482-1414

Cool Features: Huge servings of delicious eggs, pancakes, and breakfast stuff, always tons of leftovers, great hangover cure

Price: $5–$10

Hours: Daily 6 a.m.–3 p.m.

Bucca di Beppo

Food: Italian

505 W. Foothill Blvd.

(909) 399-3287

Cool Features: Huge family-style portions. Go with a big group.

Price: $15–$25

Hours: Daily 4 p.m.–10 p.m.

Buffalo Wild Wings

Food: Wings and beer

8188 Day Creek Blvd.

(909) 899-9832

Cool Features: Neat sports bar atmosphere, specializing in finger foods, great wings selection, nice low-key atmosphere

Price: $6 for wings

Hours: Daily 11 a.m.–2 a.m.

Casa De Salsa

Food: Mexican

415 W. Foothill Blvd.

(909) 445-1200

Cool Features: $1 tacos and $2 margaritas on Mondays, jazz on Tuesdays

Price: $5 on Monday nights; $10–$15 otherwise

Hours: Sunday–Thursday 11:30 a.m.–9:30 p.m., Friday–Saturday 11:30 a.m.–10 p.m.

China Star

Food: Chinese

921 Foothill Blvd.

(909) 624-2328

Cool Features: The area seriously lacks good Chinese food, but this is the best.

Price: $5–$8

Hours: Daily 11 a.m.–10 p.m.

Chipotle
Food: Mexican
1092 Mountain Ave.
(909) 579-0999
Cool Features: Kind of silly with all the good Mexican around, but still good burritos
Price: $6–$10
Hours: Daily 11 a.m.–10 p.m.

Claremont Juice Company
Food: Healthy
124 Yale Ave.
(909) 626-2216
Price: $5–$10
Hours: Monday–Saturday
7 a.m.–7 p.m.,
Sunday 8 a.m.–4 p.m.

Eddie's New York Pizza
Food: Pizza
1065 Foothill Blvd.
(909) 368-1985
Price: $7–$20
Hours: Sunday–Thursday
11 a.m.–9 p.m., Friday–
Saturday 11 a.m.–10 p.m.

Elephant Bar
Food: Asian-American fusion
4949 S. Plaza Inn
(909) 621-3509
Cool Features: Good drinks
Price: $12–$18
Hours: Daily 11 a.m.–11 p.m.

Full of Life
Food: Fresh bread and sandwiches
333 West Bonita Ave.
(909) 624-3420
Cool Features: Great gourmet deli sandwiches
Price: $5–$8 sandwiches
Hours: Daily 7 a.m.–5 p.m.

Harvard Square Café
Food: American
206 W. Bonita Ave.
(909) 626-7763
Cool Features: Outdoor seating, higher quality food for good prices
Price: $15–$20
Hours: Daily 11 a.m.–9:30 p.m.

Heroes
Food: American
131 Yale Ave.
(909) 621-6712
Cool Features: Free peanuts, shells all over the floor, huge 30-ounce beers (and other drinks). Portions are gigantic, and there are always leftovers.
Price: $12–$20 food,
9-dollar 30 oz. beers
Hours: Tuesday–Sunday
5 p.m.–11 p.m.

In-N-Out Burger

Food: Burgers

1837 Foothill Blvd.

(949) 509-6200

Cool Features: World-famous fresh burgers and great fries, although admittedly an acquired taste. Get to know the secret menu. "Animal-style" comes with delicious little grilled onions.

Price: $4–$8

Hours: Sunday–Thursday 11 a.m.–12:30 a.m., Friday–Saturday 11 a.m.–1 a.m.

Juanita's Burritos

Food: Mexican

1735 Indian Hill Blvd.

(909) 624-1272

Cool Features: Huge, super-sized burritos.

Price: $8 super-sized burritos, $5 normal burritos

Hours: Daily 10:30 a.m.–7 p.m.

Mix Bowl Café

Food: Asian

1520 Indian Hill Blvd.

(909) 447-4401

Price: $5–$10

Hours: Daily 10 a.m.–2 a.m.

Mongolian BBQ

Food: Mongolian BBQ buffet—it's a fun meal, and tasty.

970 W. Foothill Blvd.

(Mongolian BBQ, continued)

(909) 624-4334

Cool Features: $10 all-you-can-eat buffet

Price: $10

Hours: Sunday–Thursday 11:30 a.m.–8:45 p.m., Friday–Saturday 11:30 a.m.–9:45 p.m.

Olive Garden

Food: Italian

9251 Monte Vista Ave.

(909) 621-0636

Cool Features: Never-ending pasta bowl, unlimited breadsticks

Price: $15 for dinner

Hours: Sunday–Thursday 11 a.m.–10 p.m., Friday–Saturday 11 a.m.–11 p.m.

Patty's Burritos

Food: Mexican

1332 N. Towne Ave.

(909) 625-9160

Price: $8 super-sized burritos, $5 normal burritos

Hours: Sunday–Friday 11 a.m.–8 p.m., Saturday 11 a.m.–4 p.m.

Pizza and Such

Food: Pizza

202 Yale Ave.

(909) 624-7214

Price: $10–$20

(Pizza and Such, continued)
Hours: Sunday–Thursday
11 a.m.–9 p.m., Friday–
Saturday 11 a.m.–10 p.m.

Shogun
Food: Japanese
2123 Foothill Blvd.
(909) 596-9393
Cool Features: Sushi train
in one half and a hibachi
steakhouse in the other
Price: $2–$5 sushi train,
$18–$20 hibachi dinners
Hours: Daily 11:30 a.m.–
10 p.m.

Some Crust
Food: Bakery
119 Yale Ave.
(909) 621-9772
Price: $5–$10
Hours: Monday–Friday
6:30 a.m.–6 p.m.,
Saturday 7 a.m.–6 p.m.,
Sunday 7:30 a.m.–1:30 p.m.

Sushi Cruise
Food: Sushi
962 W Foothill Blvd.
(909) 398-4415
Cool Features: All you can eat
for $25
Price: $5–$25
Hours: Daily 11:30 a.m.–
2:30 p.m., 5 p.m.–10 p.m.

Tasty Goody
Food: Chinese
1630 W. Foothill Blvd.
(909) 946-8878
Cool Features: Massively
gargantuan portions
Price: $5–$10
Hours: Daily 11 a.m.–9 p.m.

Tutti Mangia
Food: Italian
102 Harvard Ave.
(909) 625-4669
Cool Features: Good
bread, great desserts, cool
atmosphere
Price: $15–$25
Hours: Sunday–Thursday
5 a.m.–9:30 p.m., Friday–
Saturday 5 a.m.–10:30 p.m.

Viva Madrid!
Food: Tapas
225 Yale Ave.
(909) 624-5500
Price: $10–$20
Hours: Tuesday–Sunday
5 p.m.–11 p.m.

Walter's
Food: Afghan
316 Yale Ave.
(909) 624-2779
Price: $10–$18
Hours: Monday–Saturday
7 a.m.–9 p.m.,
Sunday 8 a.m.–9 p.m.

Other Places to Check Out:

Buffalo Inn

Del Taco

Domino's Pizza

The Elephant Bar

Everest

Legends

The Press

Starbucks

Taco Nazo

Tacos Mexicos

Victoria Gardens

Yanni's Greek Restaurant

Wendy's

Student Favorites:

Aladdin Jr.

Full of Life

Heroes

In-N-Out Burger

Some Crust

Grocery Stores:

AM/PM Mini Mart

(909) 445-9654

701 E. Foothill Blvd.

Ralph's Grocery Company

835 W. Foothill Blvd.

(909) 625-2659

Wolfe's Market

160 W. Foothill Blvd.

(909) 626-8508

24-Hour Dining:

AM/PM convenience store, a few of the fast food places.

Best Breakfast:

42nd St. Bagel

BC Cafe

Best Chinese:

China Star (for quality)

Tasty Goody (for quantity)

Best Healthy:

Claremont Juice Co.

Full of Life

Best Pizza:

Eddie's New York Pizza

Pizza n' Such

Best Wings:

Buffalo Wild Wings

Best Place to Take Your Parents:

Aruffo's

Tutti Mangi

Viva Madrid

Walter's

Students Speak Out On...
Off-Campus Dining

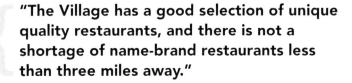

{ **"The Village has a good selection of unique quality restaurants, and there is not a shortage of name-brand restaurants less than three miles away."**

Q "There is a Spanish tapas restaurant in the Village called Viva Madrid. **Heroes is excellent for a chill night**. Of course, Some Crust is my favorite. The Claremont Juice Company has an excellent drink called McKenna Beach (and good sandwiches). It's a little pricey, though. Everything in the Village is a little pricey, but it's all well worth it."

Q "**Great food**. Harvard Square Café, Sushi Cruise, and good Italian restaurants."

Q "The Village has some nice offerings, but **most are a little above the student budget**. Fast food reigns supreme in the other surrounding areas, with Del Taco, In-N-Out Burger, Domino's Pizza, and Mix Bowl dominating. Other favorites are Sushi Cruise, Patty's Burritos, and Tacos Mexicos. Generally, Mexican and Asian food is pretty good, because it's Southern California."

Q "Yanni's Greek restaurant, Tutti Mangi, and Aruffo's are the **best in the Village**."

Q "The restaurants in the Village are good, but a bit expensive. As you move farther away from the Village, there are a number of cheaper options. **21 Choices Frozen Yogurt** on Foothill is an obvious favorite for college students."

Q "**Restaurants off campus are great**. There are the normal chains (Buca Di Beppo, Olive Garden, the Elephant Bar) and there are also great restaurants in the Village, particularly Harvard Square Café. Also, the Claremont Juice Company makes the best smoothies."

Q "Go to Victoria Gardens—it's 15–20 minutes away on the 210 East, and there's a lot of really good food around there. **It's worth leaving campus**."

Q "For good eats, **my favorites are the Mongolian BBQ place**, Eddie's New York Pizza, and Patty's Burritos."

Q "If you drive towards Ontario, you will hit pretty much every fast food franchise you could imagine. In-and-Out and Chipotle are pretty popular among CMC students. Taco Nazo has 99-cent fish taco nights. In the Village there are a lot of nice restaurants like Walter's and Harvard Square Café, which are good for dates or to take visiting relatives. **Heroes in the Village has good burgers**. There are also a lot of good places for coffee or light snacks, like Claremont Juice Company (which has smoothies named after the various Claremont colleges) 42nd Street Bagel, Some Crust, and of course, the token Starbucks."

Q "**Restaurants are great off campus**. For burgers and stuff, there's always In-N-Out, but try Everest or Legends. The Buffalo Inn has the best atmosphere for a really casual outdoor dinner, Sushi Cruise is great sushi, the Press is nice for more formal stuff, and Pasadena and LA aren't that far away if you want to eat somewhere cool."

Q "The Claremont Village has a **great selection of unique and delicious restaurants**, most of which will be brand-new to incoming students because there are very few chains. Dining options range from Italian to Middle Eastern to American hamburgers. Claremont is also close to all the College fast-food favorites, and many of these restaurants deliver on campus."

The College Prowler Take On...
Off-Campus Dining

Suburban Los Angeles provides a huge variety of great places to eat on a college budget, from everyday burrito and sushi places to upscale places to go with your family on parents weekend. The Village is closest to campus, but is the least budget-friendly area around. On the cheaper end, there is Heroes, a great sports bar with huge portions and giant beers, and a good pizza place. There are a few good but pricey sandwich places for lunch. When the parental units come to town, take them to Viva Madrid, a great Tapas bar, Walter's, an Afghani place, or either of the two upscale Italian places. Near campus in other directions just about every culture is represented, from Mongolian barbeque to Middle Eastern. Mexican, Chinese, and Japanese are particularly well represented. There is a sushi place on nearly every block. Fast food is also well represented, with every major brand within a few miles, including the much-worshipped In-N-Out.

The Claremont Colleges are just a small blip on the radar screen of the San Bernadino, so not many places do college-oriented specials, but there are some great happy hour food and drink specials around for students willing to poke their nose around a bit. Casa de Salsa's dollar taco, two-dollar margarita Mondays are one example. In summary, it's not hard to eat on a budget, just go to Heroes for giant beers, only order pizza from Roundtable if you absolutely have to, and avoid the Hot Dog Pad Thai at Mix Bowl.

The College Prowler® Grade on

Off-Campus Dining: A-

A high Off-Campus Dining grade implies that off-campus restaurants are affordable, accessible, and worth visiting. Other factors include the variety of cuisine and the availability of alternative options (vegetarian, vegan, kosher).

Campus Housing

The Lowdown On...
Campus Housing

Undergrads Living on Campus:
94%

Number of Dormitories:
12

Number of University-Owned Apartments:
36

Best Dorms:
Appleby

Worst Dorms:
Auen
Berger
Phillips

Freshmen Required to Live on Campus?
Yes

→

Dormitories:

North Quad:

Appleby

Floors: 2

Number of Occupants: 71

Bathrooms: 1 per suite

Coed: Yes

Residents: Freshmen and upperclassmen

Room Types: Suites

Special Features: Conference room lounge with soda machine and mini kitchen, good for doing work during the day, and the conference tables are perfectly sized for Beruit at night. Can be loud since it's usually only a step or two away from the on-campus parties.

Boswell

Floors: 2

Number of Occupants: 71

Bathrooms: One per suite

Coed: Yes

Residents: Freshmen and upperclassmen

Room Types: Suites

Special Features: Nice new lounge setup for group study, has a mini-kitchen.
Can be loud since it's usually only a step or two away from the on-campus parties.

Green

Floors: 2

Number of Occupants: 71

Bathrooms: One per suite

Coed: Yes

Residents: Freshmen and upperclassmen (especially athletes)

Room Types: Suites

Special Features: Lounge on each floor. Game room lounge with pool table and sweet couches.

Wohlford

Floors: 2

Number of Occupants: 71

Bathrooms: One per suite

Coed: Yes

Residents: Freshmen and upperclassmen

Room Types: Suites

Special Features: Lounge on each floor, big screen TV in lounge

Mid Quad:

Beckett

Floors: 2

Number of Occupants: 65

Bathrooms: 4

Coed: Yes

Residents: Freshmen and upperclassmen

Room Types: Singles and doubles

Special Features: Lounge with air hockey table, coed floors

Benson

Floors: 3

Number of Occupants: 80

Bathrooms: 3

Coed: Yes

Residents: Freshmen and upperclassmen

Room Types: Singles and doubles

Special Features: Ping-Pong and pool tables, main lounge, mini lounge, air-conditioned

Berger

Floors: 2

Number of Occupants: 70

Bathrooms: 2

Coed: Yes

Residents: Freshmen and upperclassmen

Room Types: Singles and doubles

Special Features: Pool table, big TV in upstairs lounge

Marks

Floors: 3

Number of Occupants: 75

Bathrooms: 6

Coed: Yes

Residents: Freshmen and upperclassmen

Room Types: Doubles and singles

Special Features: Air-conditioned. Singles have huge bay windows overlooking campus. One of the few dorms with co-ed floors. Big lounge.

Phillips

Floors: 2

Number of Occupants: 70

Bathrooms: 2

Coed: Yes

Residents: Freshmen and upperclassmen

Room Types: Doubles and singles

Special Features: Lounge on each floor, directly across from the dining hall.

South Quad:

Auen

Floors: 7

Number of Occupants: 76

Bathrooms: 7

Coed: Yes

Residents: Freshmen and upperclassmen

Room Types: Doubles, singles, and a quad

Special Features: Air conditioned, with lounge on each floor. Live in one of the three tallest buildings in Claremont! Quieter than most dorms.

Fawcett

Floors: 7

Number of Occupants: 76

Bathrooms: 6

Coed: Yes

Residents: Freshmen and upperclassmen

Room Types: Doubles, singles, and a quad

(Fawcett, continued)

Special Features: Air-conditioned, with lounge on each floor. Live in one of the three tallest buildings in Claremont! Quieter than most dorms. Great views.

Stark

Floors: 7

Number of Occupants: 80

Bathrooms: 14

Coed: Yes

Residents: Freshmen and upperclassmen

Room Types: Singles and doubles

Special Features: Substance-free, air-conditioned, computer lab, big screen TV, foosball table and Ping-Pong table in lounge. Rooms are massive.

Student Apartment Complex

Floors: 2–3 per building

Number of Occupants: 144

Bathrooms: Two per apartment

Coed: Yes

Residents: Upperclassmen

Room Types: Four singles per apartment

Special Features: Full kitchen, barbeque areas, volleyball and basketball courts adjacent, student residents not required to be on the meal plan

Housing Offered:

Singles: 40%

Doubles: 47%

Triples/Suites: 0%

Apartments: 13%

Room Types

Singles – Dorm rooms with one bed and one occupant

Doubles – Dorm rooms with two beds and two occupants

Quads – A few lounges have been turned into 4-occupant rooms; used mainly for transfers

Suites – North Quad dorms are all suite-style with 4 double rooms connected through a private double bathroom

Apartments – 4-bedroom, 2-bathroom apartments with full kitchen and living room

Bed Type

Twin extra-long

Also Available

Lawn chairs free of charge

Cleaning Service

Yes, regular bathroom cleanup and individual room cleanup every two weeks

What You Get

Bed, dresser, desk, bookshelf, bureau, hardwire Internet port, trash cans, lawn chairs

Students Speak Out On...
Campus Housing

"All of the dorms are very spacious. There aren't really dorms to avoid on campus unless you are looking for a particular social scene."

Q "**The dorms are huge**—I really like the motel-suite style of North Quad."

Q "CMC has a **great selection of dorms** that fit a variety of personalities."

Q "Rooms are about as spacious as college dorms get. The bathrooms are clean. We have regular maid service. Every dorm also has a lounge which is pretty nice. North Quad tends to be more popular because it is more social, due to the emphasis on out-of-doors built into the design. **South Quad tends to be a lot more quiet** and for the studiously-minded. Mid Quad is a happy balance of both."

Q "Dorms are great, a lot bigger than most other schools' I've seen. Avoid Mid Quad because those dorms are ugly (except for Benson, that's nice). **North Quad is for parties**, and South Quad is for studiers. I'm in the Student Apartments, which are fantastic."

Q "**All of the dorms are very spacious**. There aren't really dorms to avoid on campus unless you are looking for a particular social scene."

Q "Spend your freshman year in North Quad, preferably Green or Appleby. That will maximize your party experience, you may want to stay—or you may realize you're antisocial and would rather live in Mid Quad. The towers (especially Fawcett) can actually be a very wet and wild place—and **you can have a single there**, too."

Q "I've lived in Berger, Phillips, and Beckett. I liked them all—there was nothing wrong with any of them, but in the end, **I preferred living in Beckett** because girls can live on the first floor, which makes moving in and out much easier."

Q "I don't like North Quad; it has **no air-conditioning and no privacy**. I love Stark, but it is so antisocial I will never live there again; Mid and South Quads are nice, but they get gross on the weekends."

Q "**Socially, North Quad is really an amazing place** to live. People keep their doors open all day, lay out on the grass on warm days, barbeque, and it is just a really open and friendly place. North Quad is also renowned for its party scene, and thus living there comes with a sense of pride. The rumor is that North Quad residents party harder, party louder, and party longer. And the rumor is true."

Q "Living in North Quad comes at a price. **It is always loud during the weekends**, and often loud during the weeknights. As an athlete with morning practice my freshman year, the noise could be frustrating. North Quad residents sometimes have to find alternative places to study. The study lounges are occupied for Beirut on weekends, weeknights, and even during finals week. The library and reading room end up being better places to go and do work."

Q "I would say there are very few dorms to systematically avoid, as each dorm tends to have its own feel, which will appeal to different individuals. **My favorite dorm on campus is Stark**, the substance-free dorm. The atmosphere is conducive to studying, and it is the newest dorm on campus with some of the largest rooms. However, others might say that Stark is too quiet and a dorm to avoid. Unfortunately, I know several people who heeded this warning when they entered as freshmen and requested dorms other than Stark, only later to regret not having requested Stark, because it truly is the dorm where they fit in the best. I would say there are no dorms to avoid unconditionally, just dorms that certain people would not fit into well."

Q "**I'm not so sure I would necessarily recommend living in North Quad as a freshman**, because I think the majority of freshman live in Mid or South Quad, and so you end up getting mixed in with upperclassmen—which can be good or bad. My freshman year, I lived in a suite with junior girls who had just returned from study abroad. Re-acclimating to CMC after a study abroad experience can be difficult. The smallness of it can feel oppressive to someone who has been traveling the world. The girls were pretty negative about the CMC scene, and it was difficult as a freshman to hear their criticism at a time when I was seeking confirmation that I made the right college choice."

Q "All of CMC's housing is **spacious and well-kept**. CMC also offers several different types of dorms to fit the students' different personalities and preferences. You can have an outdoor balcony if you want, or you can live in an air-conditioned room. Some dorms have lounges right outside the bedrooms, others connect directly to bathrooms. There are also plenty of singles on campus for upperclassmen who want one."

Q "It really is a matter of taste. Some people love North Quad, despite the fact that it has no air-conditioning. Personally, **I prefer South Quad dorms** (except for Stark) because a) they're the cleanest since nobody really parties there, b) they're the quietest, c) they have a common room on each floor that is more conducive to social activity with the rest of your floor, and d) the singles are bigger. You can party in North Quad, and go back to Auen or Fawcett to sleep and relax."

Q "**I think the dorms are great**. I'm in Mid Quad (Phillips). The showers are kind of gross, but my roommate and I got put in a triple just for us, so our room is huge."

The College Prowler Take On...
Campus Housing

Because a vast majority of students live on campus, dorm quality is a high priority at Claremont. Residence halls are split evenly into four different areas: North, Mid and South Quads, and the Student Apartments. North Quadders live in suites with four double rooms connected around the bathroom. Mid Quad dorms are the most traditional, with singles and doubles arranged along hall ways with big central bathrooms for each floor. South Quad dorms are tall, with 12 residents in singles and doubles on each floor sharing a bathroom and a central lounge. The Student Apartments house mainly seniors in four-person apartments and are located on the far side of campus. North Quad hosts most of the on-campus parties and tends to be a loud place to live—South Quad is relatively quiet, and Mid Quad flip-flops in between. South Quad dorms, one Mid Quad dorm, and the Apartments are the only air-conditioned housing. Dorm rooms are roomy, especially doubles, and adjustable furniture allows students to make space by lofting their beds to different heights. Stark Hall, the substance-free dorm, has by far the biggest and nicest rooms, but residents are obviously subject to a substance-free living agreement.

Freshmen are generally assigned doubles with freshman roommates based on a housing survey upon acceptance. Students can request preferred quads on this sheet as well. Mid Quad is a great place for freshmen to live, because the dorm setup makes it really easy to meet a lot of people quickly, and the atmosphere is rarely too loud or too quiet.

The College Prowler® Grade on

Campus Housing: A-

A high Campus Housing grade indicates that dorms are clean, well-maintained, and spacious. Other determining factors include variety of dorms, proximity to classes, and social atmosphere.

Off-Campus Housing

The Lowdown On...
Off-Campus Housing

Undergrads in Off-Campus Housing:
6%

Average Rent For:
Studio: $900 per month
1-BR Apt.: $1,050 per month
2-BR Apt.: $1,200 per month

Popular Areas:
Nowhere specific is any more popular than anywhere else; just find yourself a development with a pool.

For Assistance Contact:
CMC doesn't provide any assistance for finding off-campus housing, but the San Francisco Bay Area on Craigslist is a good first place to check: *www.craigslist.org/sfc*

Students Speak Out On...
Off-Campus Housing

"Stay on campus as long as you can, because it is so much a part of the experience. However, if ever necessary, there is off-campus housing across the street from Harvey Mudd."

Q "No one lives off campus. I would say don't live off campus. **You'll miss out on CMC life**."

Q "**Not worth it**; we are a residential college. Stay on campus."

Q "Our school's staff/administrators are extremely unaccommodating when it comes to alternate senior housing. Granted, I'm sure they deal with millions of complaints from seniors every year, but the fact is that **they don't help us** or give us any suggestions whatsoever."

Q "I am still really upset with the way we were treated when we did not get an apartment. Not only was it horrible to find out that we would not be living among the rest of our senior class, we had no idea where to live, and **no one at CMC would help us**."

Q "I do enjoy my living situation this year, because it is **awesome to have a 'home' to go home to**, particularly such a nice one. It is also nice to have a quiet place to work, sleep, and relax, where you know you will not be interrupted by drunken 18-year-olds puking in the bushes outside your window."

Q "People generally only live off campus for financial reasons, or if they are forced to because they do not get into the apartments on campus their senior year. However, **I currently live off campus, and I love it**, with the exception of driving back and forth every day. It is nice to have a place away from campus to call home, but it does sometimes feel like there are things going on on campus that you might be missing out on."

Q "**Almost every student lives on campus**, and because the Claremont area is generally expensive, few students live off campus after freshman year."

Q "**Most people don't look into living off campus**, but it is definitely available right north of the 5C's."

Q "**CMC guarantees housing all four years**, and most people take that route. Off-campus housing is fairly cheap and (I think) easy to find, but the CMC community is so strongly rooted on campus that one can feel disconnected being off-campus. Also, a car is definitely necessary if you live off campus."

The College Prowler Take On...
Off-Campus Housing

Off-campus housing is not a popular option at Claremont. Housing is assured for all four years, and few people pass up the chance to live in the middle of everything. For those who do choose to live off campus, there is little help. Sometimes names of good apartment complexes are handed down from class to class, but there is no such thing as a "students area" off campus, only a few random apartments scattered here and there. Most of the areas around campus are safe to live in, and affordable housing can be found just a few minutes from school. Living in an apartment off of the meal plan is almost surely a savings if you don't factor in car-related costs that are required for the drive to school.

It's not that students can't live off campus, it's just simply that they don't. There are one or two groups of friends who move out every year, but they become very separated from all of the activities that go on at school. The dorms are comfortable, and the food is good, so there is no desperate need to get out, and come senior year, most students have the option of moving out to the Student Apartment Complex, which provides all the joys of living off campus while still staying within the Claremont McKenna bubble.

The College Prowler® Grade on

Off-Campus Housing: D

A high grade in Off-Campus Housing indicates that apartments are of high quality, close to campus, affordable, and easy to secure.

Diversity

The Lowdown On...
Diversity

African American:
4%

Native American:
<1%

Asian American:
15%

White:
64%

Hispanic:
12%

Unknown:
0%

International:
4%

Out-of-State:
50%

Political Activity

Claremont is a unique place; the student body is split almost equally along the political spectrum, which makes for some very good debates. A lot of students are politically active, a vast majority of students are passionate about some issue, and everyone is well informed.

Gay Pride

Claremont's student body is relatively laid-back, but sexual orientation makes more CMC students uncomfortable than any other diversity issue. That being said, there is a significant gay population at the five colleges, and being openly gay at CMC isn't an issue, although some individuals admit to feeling uncomfortable. There is a large and well supported Straight But Not Narrow group at Claremont and a Queer Resource Center available to all Consortium students.

Economic Status

Because CMC gives such generous financial aid, students come from all different walks of life and no one gives economic background a second thought. The school subsidizes the cost of many activities, which allows everyone in the student body to participate.

Minority Clubs

Asian Students Club, Black Student Union, Empowered Black Women, Empowered Latinos/as in Action, Hillel, Jewish Student Union, Muslim Students Association, Office of Black Student Affairs, Pan-African Student Association, Queer Questioning Allied Mentoring Program, Queer Resource Center, Straight But Not Narrow, Taiwanese Student Union, TRANScend, Women's Forum

Most Common Religions

Christianity is the dominant religion at Claremont and is an active community, but there is also a high percentage of Jewish students, and there aren't any religious tolerance issues. InterVarsity, the Christian organization on campus is the largest organization in the Consortium.

Students Speak Out On...
Diversity

"**Politically and ideologically, CMC is very diverse. As a school known for government majors, we draw a wide range of interests and views and are constantly debating all sorts of topics.**"

Q "Our political diversity is **fantastic**."

Q "CMC is not the most diverse place in the world on any level, but definite steps are being taken to change this. In addition, the other schools at the 5Cs definitely add the different levels to the diversity. So, in the end, you come up with a **political, sexual, and ideological diversity**— ethnic and economic diversity are still a bit lacking."

Q "The campus is **lacking in diversity**."

Q "Many students entering college are religious, and **some will even avoid a school like CMC** that seems to be profoundly secular or even hostile to their faith. Yet some of these students might be better fits than they think, if they only knew the full picture."

Q "I don't think anyone will feel like they can't **find a home at CMC**."

Q "About **as diverse as any college**, although thankfully not all the students are liberal (I'd say a 60/40 liberal/conservative split), which is really good for engaging in debate."

Q "CMC has the reputation for being **quite conservative**. In my experience, however, I would say there is about a 50-50 split on the campus between conservative and liberal students. This makes CMC seem conservative in comparison to most colleges, where the dominant political view is liberal. Therefore, I believe that CMC is much more politically diverse than most schools; it's by no means overrun by conservative thought."

Q "Economically, I would say **we're probably average**— a solid representation of people from lower-income backgrounds, but not enough to say we are very economically diverse. We have an excellent financial aid program, though, so we try really hard in this category."

Q "I went to a public school composed very differently from CMC. **It was more ethnically diverse** with more students from a lower socio-economic status."

Q "Economically, sexually, and ethnically, CMC is not very diverse. This is probably **one of CMC's major drawbacks**. Because of the smallness of its student body, you don't get the same level of diversity you would find at a UC. However, CMC has a great ideological and political culture. It has a reputation for being conservative, but the truth is it just has more conservatives than the average college campus. Because most college campuses are overwhelmingly liberal, to say that CMC has more conservatives than average isn't saying much. Rather, I think we have a great balance. There are strong viewpoints on both ends of the political spectrum, and the constant debate that ensues both in classes and in campus life makes CMC truly unique."

Q "CMC, Scripps, and Mudd have a large, active, vibrant, diverse, joyful, and theologically sound **Christian fellowship**, which is either the largest club registered at CMC or pretty close to it."

Q "There is a very, very small homosexual community on CMC's campus. People who are gay usually have to go to one of the other colleges to find prospective boy/girlfriends. Ethnically, we are probably about average in terms of diversity. **We are very white**, but we make a solid effort to be aware of diversity. As a student who is from New York City, I feel that CMC is pretty white, but most colleges are (unfortunately)."

Q "Politically, almost split in the middle. Economically, most come from upper-middle-class homes. Sexually, not quite sure (definitely a mix, though). Ethnically, I think CMC is **one of the most diverse campuses in the nation** (and I am Hispanic). CMC does an excellent job (and continues to improve) recruiting minorities through programs like JEAMMA (John E. Allen Alumni Merit Award)."

The College Prowler Take On...
Diversity

Claremont's minority enrollment statistics don't lie: Claremont does not rank above average on ethnic diversity. However, its financial aid stats don't lie either—CMCers come from many different socioeconomic backgrounds. Claremont students are smart, with the ability to argue and debate while still respecting another person's point of view, which gives everyone the freedom to be different. Of all diversity issues, CMCers are probably most uncomfortable with sexual orientation. While there isn't any hostility towards gay or lesbian students, it is definitely the hottest diversity issue on campus.

In the spring of 2004, there was one major incident in which a professor's car was vandalized with hate slang and bashed in, but it turned out that the (now former) professor had done it to her own car, because she thought students at the Five Colleges were too complacent. The students proved her wrong, however, when over 4,000 students came out to a day-long rally protesting hate crimes and supporting the professor. Claremont students care about tolerance, but because people so rarely disrespect others, it isn't an everyday issue. Because Claremont students come from all over the country and all over the world, and from many different backgrounds, Claremont McKenna is a school where people learn about other people and other ways of life and new ideas. You would be hard-pressed to find a student here who isn't friends with someone who has vastly different beliefs.

The College Prowler® Grade on

Diversity: B+

A high grade in Diversity indicates that ethnic minorities and international students have a notable presence on campus and that students of different economic backgrounds, religious beliefs, and sexual preferences are well-represented.

Guys & Girls

The Lowdown On...
Guys & Girls

Male Undergrads:
54%

Female Undergrads:
46%

Birth Control Available?
Yes, at the Baxter Health Center

Social Scene
Claremont has a very active social scene, based mostly on campus. Campus parties are put on by the Student Government, and alcohol is relatively free-flowing. Parties range in size from small dorm get-togethers to school-wide parties to Five College parties.

(Social Scene, continued)

Not everyone parties, but you'll find mostly empty rooms on weekends since the student body is really outgoing and there are a lot of alternatives to the typical party like club events and IM sports.

Hookups or Relationships?

There is a pretty even balance between people in some sort of serious relationship and people out looking for booty at parties and such. Random hookups are common, and although not everyone will know your business, do remember that it can be a very small community at times.

Best Places to Meet Guys/Girls

Parties on campus are the main vehicle for love, and loose keg taps provide a social lubricant for a lot of people. But parties usually have a theme, and major points go to the most creative or funny, rather than those who can drink the most. There's nothing sexy about a sloppy drunk. Most weekends, there are Five College parties, which are big and are definitely the best place for a promiscuous chance encounter. Claremont throws good parties, although quantity is more our forte, while Harvey Mudd throws the wildest bashes. Scripps (the all-girls school) is always a good place to find girls, and any of the colleges can be hunting ground for guys (although Mudders sometimes have a reputation for social ineptness).

For anyone not looking for the magical moment that is a drunken hookup, the sky is the limit on good places to meet people. A lot of CMCers would label the brain as the sexiest organ, so it's not completely unheard of to meet people in class, or, more likely, at a club event. Mudd hosts the Occasional Ball from time to time, which is a dry party with free ballroom dancing lessons, which are fun.

Dress Code

Dress is really relaxed, with flip-flops the only uniform. CMCers are pretty typical college kids wearing clothes ranging from good thrift store pick-ups to the prep-lite styles of Abercrombie, Hollister, and J.Crew. Since so many people play sports, athletic wear is common, too. At parties, people often dress for the theme, such as Smilin' 80s. CMC dresses more conservatively than most of the consortium, but around the 5Cs it's not out of the question to see guys in kilts and anything else you can think of.

Did You Know?

Top Three Places to Find Hotties:

1. Scripps Pool (both guys and girls use the pool, which is the nicest of the 5Cs)
2. Green Beach on a warm day
3. Five-College Party

Top Five Places to Hook Up:

1. Screw Your Roommate Party (no, not like that— your roomie sets you up on a blind date)
2. Trick or Drink
3. Mardi Gras
4. Toga Party
5. Anywhere near the keg

Students Speak Out On...
Guys & Girls

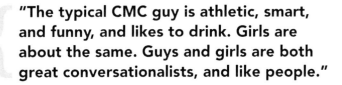

"The typical CMC guy is athletic, smart, and funny, and likes to drink. Girls are about the same. Guys and girls are both great conversationalists, and like people."

Q "Guys are like guys anywhere: some are kinda cute, some are kinda dorky, most aren't looking for any serious relationships. I would say the guys here are hot, but I have been told I have low standards, so I don't know. The girls here are average to hot. Because **so many people are athletic and friendly**, it makes for a good social scene. There is not much dating, mostly just random hooking up and a few serious relationships. The typical student is fun, friendly, smart, and very involved."

Q "On average, the girls aren't terribly sexy, and most forget what it's like to dress up (you'll rarely see Claremont ladies wearing heels to class). Most guys and gals readily adopt the laid-back Hollister/Abercrombie fashion of board shorts and flip-flops. Regardless of what they're wearing, **everyone is always friendly** and more than willing to lend a hand or a red cup."

Q "There are hot girls and guys, and there are not-so-hot girls and guys. The range is definitely out there. A typical student would be a good-looking, bring-home-to-the-family type, but **nothing to swoon over** for days."

Q "I think CMCers have a little bit of that old-fashioned *Animal House* craziness in them, but tempered with a big goofy streak and a lot of intelligence. CMC kids **go to great lengths to find new ways to have fun**, and over-the-top is almost a way of life."

Q "When I first came to tour CMC's campus my senior year in high school, I noticed that the guys were total babes. Unfortunately, after about two years at CMC, all the hot guys left, and we were pretty much stuck with **very average guys**. Who knows, though—every class is different."

Q "**The typical CMC guy is a white econ-accounting major from California** or the West Coast; plays a fall sport, drinks heavily, wears polo shirts, skateboards—a laid-back guy. The typical girl wears denim skirts and flip-flops, drinks heavily, is a gov major, and takes care of herself. CMC people are attractive."

Q "People are **laid-back, funny, and athletic**. Some of the girls are superficial, but a lot are really chill and so much fun to hang out with."

Q "To me coming to CMC was like stepping into an Abercrombie and Fitch catalogue. The style is stereotypically preppy, more upper-middle-class white than what I was used to. **It was sort of culture shock for me**. Now I'm more accustomed to it. I would say that there are just lots of average-looking people at CMC."

Q "The guys and girls alike seem to be averse to dating and **prone to hooking up**. The campus as a whole is beautiful, with some being exceptionally beautiful (as in any place). I don't think there is a typical student, but very few are overweight. Both the girls and the guys take care of each other; you rarely have to worry about your safety when around other CMCers."

Q "Guys and girls at CMC are different from the stereotypical spring break frat boys and sorority girls. We like to party and drink, but our priorities are different, and **you won't find girls in wet T-shirt contests** or guys shooting bottle rockets out of bodily orifices. Getting skunked in Beruit does invoke the naked rule, but that's about as crazy as it gets."

Q "People are **very social** here."

Q "**The girls are cute**, but then again, you kinda get CMC goggles after a while, where everyone starts looking better by comparison. Make sure to get out from time to time!"

Q "CMC guys and girls both are a great mix of people. I like how laid-back CMC is, because it makes meeting people even easier. **You can casually meet tons of people** or find someone to date seriously, and students take advantage of both these options."

Q "There are a lot of attractive girls here. The problem is most of these cute girls know that they are cute. So they are aware that they are in high demand. I'd say that a typical student is **intelligent, athletic, and competitive**."

Q "I would say **CMC girls are particularly cute**—they are smart and witty, not to mention damn sexy."

The College Prowler Take On...
Guys & Girls

Despite Claremont's academic reputation and sometimes ambitious workload, what sets it apart from similar schools is the outgoing nature of its student body. CMCers like to get out and meet people, whether it's at a party, a concert, a movie, or any other social event. That means tons of chances to meet the one—or just someone, depending on who you're looking for. CMCers dabble in both the one-night stand and the long-term commitment. Most people are single, which means meeting a random stranger at a party isn't abnormal. On the flipside, while CMCers don't marry as a rule, it happens often enough not to seem unusual. The five colleges in the Claremont consortium provide a deep pool of all different types of people with hugely varied interests, so there isn't just one type who can find love or lovin', and you'll never run the risk of meeting everyone if you look around. One thing you won't find at CMC is the *Girls Gone Wild* film crew prowling the parties. CMC guys and girls don't do much public nudity, and parties don't usually center on sex as much as other types of debauchery (although you might get lucky on Mardi Gras weekend).

Most RAs keep a stock of condoms for those who didn't plan ahead (and earplugs for their neighbors). The Health Education Outreach, located in the health center, also provides free condoms and other contraceptives, in addition to a wealth of information on everything you should know about safe hookups, and for gosh sakes, people, if you're gonna do it, do it safe!

The College Prowler® Grade on
Guys: B+

A high grade for Guys indicates that the male population on campus is attractive, smart, friendly, and engaging, and that the school has a decent ratio of guys to girls.

The College Prowler® Grade on
Girls: A-

A high grade for Girls not only implies that the women on campus are attractive, smart, friendly, and engaging, but also that there is a fair ratio of girls to guys.

Athletics

The Lowdown On...
Athletics

Athletic Division:
NCAA Division III

Conference:
Southern California
Intercollegiate Athletic
Association

Colors:
Maroon and gold

School Mascot:
Athenas (women)
Stags (men)

→

Men's Varsity Sports:

Basketball
Baseball
Cross-Country
Football
Golf
Soccer
Swimming
Tennis
Track & Field
Water Polo

Women's Varsity Sports:

Baseketball
Cross-Country
Lacrosse
Soccer
Softball
Swimming
Tennis
Track & Field
Volleyball
Water Polo

Club Sports:

Crew
Cycling
Field Hockey
Lacrosse (Men's)
Rugby (Men's and Women's)
Ultimate Frisbee (Men's and Women's)
Volleyball (Men's)

Intramurals:

3-on-3 Basketball
BASEketball
Basketball
Basketball Skills
Beach Volleyball
Belly Flop Contest
Billiards
Bowling
Dodgeball
Fantasy Football
Flag Football
Golf
Homerun Derby
Hot Dog Eating
Inner Tube Water Polo
Lawn Sports Olympics
Madden Tourney
March Madness Pool
NFL Pool
One-on-One Basketball
Paintball
Pie Eating
Pumpkin Carving
Scrabble
Soccer
Swimming
Table Tennis
Tennis
Texas Hold 'Em
Track & Field
Volleyball
Wiffleball

Athletic Fields

Arce Field, CMS Aquatics Center (Matt M. Axelrood Pool), David X. Marks and Ben F. Smith Tennis Courts, Fritz Burns Stadium (Zinda Field), Pritzlaff Field Soccer Stadium, softball diamond

Getting Tickets

Tickets are free; seating is first-come, first-served.

Most Popular Sports

Football and basketball are probably the best attended sports on a regular basis. Volleyball is the best-attended women's sport. Anytime a team makes the playoffs or plays Pomona-Pitzer, the seats are full.

Best Place to Take a Walk

Hiking on Mt. Baldy, easy walks around the campuses and to the Village

Gyms/Facilities

Ducey Gym, R. Ernest Smith Weight Room, Frank G. Wells Fitness Center, rock-climbing wall, boxing ring

The Wells Fitness Center is small but adequate for the size of the school. An alumnus of the school founded the fitness equipment company LifeFitness, and he donates machines fairly regularly, so the gym is very up-to-date. The weight room, by contrast, is less up-to-date.

Students Speak Out On...
Athletics

"Varsity, club, and IM sports are all awesome. People really get into them and have a great time. Being on a team is like having a family, and the school really joins together to back the school teams."

Q "Varsity sports do fairly well. We were originally a men's college, so sports is a strong emphasis. Sports are very popular, and most students are fairly athletic if they don't play sports. **IM sports are very popular**, and some of the favorites include inner tube water polo and dodgeball."

Q "At CMC, it's nice that **varsity sports are so popular** that it doesn't put you at too much of a disadvantage academically. I opted out of participating in two sports until junior year, once I felt I had a handle on academics, but it is nice to play at a school where people are there because they want to be—there is nothing binding them to staying on the team if they want off."

Q "Varsity sports at CMC may not match up to D-I type events, but being able to know all of the athletes on the court personally makes the games **a lot of fun**."

Q "**Varsity sports are fantastic**. I can't emphasize enough how beneficial they can be to your college experience. Sports are always a great way to meet people, have fun, exercise, and to get away from academics for a while. The coaches are, in general, very personable and concerned about each person as an individual."

Q "To be perfectly honest, **varsity sports aren't that great**. IM sports might actually be better because they're so fun to watch.

Q "My varsity sport experience was **really fun, but also really intense**. Our D-III team had a workout schedule as intensive and time consuming as a lot of D-I teams. It is a great way to make friends on campus, and our teams are all pretty successful. However, I found that it was such a big-time commitment that it prevented me from participating in a lot of other awesome activities that were happening on campus. I played my freshman year and don't regret it at all. I did really well and felt it was a great accomplishment to play at the collegiate level. However, I decided my sophomore year that I had a lot of other interests and playing prevented me from exploring those."

Q "We usually **win the all sports trophies** because our teams are usually pretty good, and a high percentage of students are athletes. But no one really watches our teams, except when we play Pomona-Pitzer. IM sports are pretty popular and usually fun, like IM golf and IM inner tube waterpolo."

The College Prowler Take On...
Athletics

The California sunshine keeps Claremont's campus warm almost year-round, and many CMCers take advantage of the climate by getting outside and playing sports, from pickup bocce and four-square to Division III basketball and water polo. There is a great sports rivalry built into the Five Colleges because the schools split into two Division III teams: the Claremont-Mudd-Scripps Stags/Athena and the Pomona-Pitzer Sagehens. The stands are always packed for games between CMS and PP, and the atmosphere is electric. Other games are typically quieter, but because everyone knows athletes, there are always friends cheering on friends in the crowd. Entrance is always free, and games are easy to get into (with the exception of playoff games). For those looking for a really laid-back way to play, the school offers intramural sports almost every week in anything from inner tube water polo to paintball. One of the most popular new events is IM bowling, which happens to coincide with dollar beer night at the alley. Often, other schools in the Consortium participate, so they can be a fun way to meet people from other schools.

Claremont requires three semesters of physical education before graduation for all non-varsity athletes, but the requirement can be fun to fulfill. Options include all the normal sports like tennis and soccer, and more unique options like yoga, lifeguard training, lawn sports, playground games, sailing, and fly fishing. So while you don't have to take your sports seriously at Claremont, you are required to get out of your dorm room and enjoy the sunshine.

The College Prowler® Grade on

Athletics: B

A high grade in Athletics indicates that students have school spirit, that sports programs are respected, that games are well-attended, and that intramurals are a prominent part of student life.

Nightlife

The Lowdown On...
Nightlife

Club and Bar Prowler:
Popular Nightlife Spots!

Club Crawler:

There are no clubs in or around the Claremont area; students looking for that sort of thing can easily make the drive to LA and enjoy the scene there.

Bar Prowler:

The Buffalo Inn (The Buf)
1814 Foothill Blvd.
(909) 981-5515

The Buf has long been a student favorite for weekday happy hours (5 p.m.–7 p.m.) with delicious $2 hamburgers, homemade potato chips, and $7 pitchers with over 20 beers on tap. It's a cool bar to just sit in, an intimate little double-decker log cabin on the side of the road.

(The Buffalo Inn, continued)

When the weather is nice, there is outdoor seating around a big fire pit. The Buf is mostly a happy hour spot, but you can have a great party there or just a great meal (try the buffalo burgers).

Blackwatch

497 N. Central Ave.

(909) 981-6069

Classy is not the word to describe the Blackwatch, but if the 5Cs were to have a student bar, this would be it. It's dark, dingy, and one of the final rebellious outposts that allows smoking indoors, but make no mistake, the Blackwatch is a ton of fun. There's darts, pool, Deer Hunter, Ms. Pacman, a St. Patty's day countdown clock, and a crazy local cover band on Saturday nights. There aren't any specials to speak of, but prices are always right with $3–$5 pints and cheap pitchers every night. The Blackwatch is also one of only two bars within legitimate walking distance from campus, and although students rarely take advantage of this, it's a short seven minute stumble home should you drink too much.

The Bulldog Pub

1667 N. Mountain Ave.

(909) 946-6614

Your typical pub, kinda far from campus and nothing special. it's not particularly popular with the students.

The Cellar

195 N. Central Ave.

(909) 946-3604

The Cellar is definitely the most chic place around with a cool bar, nice lounges, and a good dance floor. As is so often true, style comes at a price and The Cellar is one of the more pricey bars around. Drink specials aren't anything special. Most people would advise you to go to LA for this kind of bar experience, although that is even more expensive.

Friar Tuck's

540 E. Foothill Blvd.

(909) 625-7265

Friar Tuck's is a pretty lowbrow bar, with a dirty feel and sticky seats. There is pool and darts, as well as a boxing ring stage for live bands. Happy hour has mediocre drink specials, although they do have free snacks like Pizza Pockets. It's not really worth the drive.

Heroes

131 N. Yale St.

(909) 621-6712

Heroes has the potential to be far and away the coolest place around, if only it stayed open later. It's a bar and grill in The Village, but it leans more towards the grill side. Still, the bar portion is great to pop into for a drink. Well, I suppose a 30-ounce beer requires more commitment than a simple pop in, but it would be hard to spend your whole night at Heroes. There are over 40 beers from around the world on tap, and you can order a big or a small (is that really an option?). It's a great place to catch a game or just hang out, although it's usually crowded with people waiting for a table, and it can be hard to get noticed.

The Press

129 Harvard Ave.

(909) 625-4808

www.thepressrestaurant.com

The Press is the only late-night venue in the Village, and it's pretty popular with students for that reason. It's classier than your typical college bar, but the prices are pretty good and there is a variety of live music many nights. Happy hour is 4 p.m.–6 p.m. on Tuesday, Wednesday, and Thursday, and every night from 10 p.m.– 12 a.m., with $4 well drinks, house wines, $3 pints and $8 pitchers.

(The Press, continued)

The beer selection is limited, but quality. The Press is the other closest bar to campus: about a 10 minute walk through Pomona's campus. Some nights the music causes a cover charge, but this happens infrequently.

Tequila Hoppers

60 N. Mountain Ave.

(909) 985-9114

Tequila Hoppers rocks. It's a great sports bar with great drink specials and waitresses who are easy on the eyes. There are TVs all over and lots of space to sit and watch a game. There is also remote poker and trivia so you can play other people around the bar. They have 80 beers, over 50 types of tequila, and great drink specials on both. There are specials every night, and from 7 p.m. to close they have deals like half off food and drinks, $1 beers, $3 you-call-its. On Sundays during football season they have specials all day long while the games are on. At night, the place gets a little wilder with live DJs and lights, making it a bit more of a dance club atmosphere. At night the clientele gets a little bit sketchy, daytime is definitely a little more enjoyable.

Other Places to Check Out:

Dave and Buster's

The Standard

Upland Bowl

The Yardhouse

Student Favorites:

The Blackwatch

The Buffalo Inn

The Press

Tequila Hoppers

Cheapest Place to Get a Drink:

Parties on campus

Primary Areas with Nightlife:

It's spread all over; there's a lot to do in LA

Bars Close At:

2 a.m.

Favorite Drinking Games:

A$$hole

Beer Die

Beruit (Beer Pong)

Edward Fortyhands

Kings

Power Hour

Speed Quarters

What to Do if You're Not 21

Aladdin Jr.'s hookah bar

Party hard on campus like everyone else

Lei parties

Students Speak Out On...
Nightlife

{ **"You cannot beat the social life that CMC has. We receive weekly e-mails describing the weekend activities, which attract people from every college."**

Q "**Parties are good**, though they tend to repeat themselves in terms of music, location, and themes."

Q "Parties on campus are great. Alcohol is usually provided, and the themes vary. Students at CMC are proud to have a strong party reputation, and we work hard to keep it that way. The other colleges throw plenty of parties, too, so if you get tired of the CMC scene, it's easy to find some other place to go. **Bars and clubs off campus aren't particularly popular**, mostly because driving is usually entailed, and that's just not safe. The threat of drunk driving is the main reason that the administration allows partying on campus."

Q "The parties vary from crappy to mediocre, with a few gems here and there. Expect to have a blast freshman year (Whee! Free booze!), and be bored of the scene after your sophomore year. Off campus, you need to go to LA—don't bother with anything else, **it's a waste of time**. I personally like the Standard on Sunset, it's a great deal. Awesome bar and lounge with reasonable bottle service."

Q "Parties on campus, for me, **got really old after a couple years**. For most people, though, it seems like the parties never get old, and there's always a great time to be had. As far as off-campus bars go, there's a few nearby, specifically the Press in the Village, that can be fun, but I'd probably drive into LA or Hollywood for a really good bar/club scene."

Q "The **parties are fantastic**, there is no way to explain it—you have to come visit."

Q "Parties on campus are good; Harvey Mudd is too crazy/freaky for me; **I am usually either at Pomona or CMC**."

Q "At CMC you will go through various phases. Because CMC is so small, **you develop a love-hate relationship** with it similar to the one most people have with their high schools. For a month you will get tired of the theme parties and seeing the same people at every party—you will abhor the Claremont Bubble. The next month you will embrace it and have an amazing time, cherishing the community intimacy."

Q "One recommendation: **Professor Ward Elliott's Singing Party**. It is an old-time CMC tradition, and it is one of my most memorable experiences at CMC."

Q "There are parties on CMC's campus at least every Thursday and Saturday, and there are parties on other campuses to fill in the voids or to bolster our own party schedule. Our school buys us beer (they're like the parents who want their kids to drink at home so they'll be safe), and they make sure that we have lots of fun by renting us things like hot tubs, mechanical bulls, and bouncy castles. **Off campus, the Buffalo Inn is best** for beer, the Press and Walters are pretty expensive but they have nice fancy drinks, and Heroes is good for big portions and giant beers. Ultimately, you could be on campus every weekend, though, and have a dandy time."

Q "CMC has the best **party scene of any campus** I know of (especially any of the other 5Cs). There is always something going on, and the parties are inclusive, not exclusive. Of course, alcohol is free but regulated. It does not matter, though; CMCers are very generous with the alcohol and cigarettes they own. I have yet to go to a bar or a club off campus (really no need to), and I have a car."

Q "**My favorite thing about CMC is how creative our on-campus parties can get**. We've had sumo wrestling parties with sake and tyko drummers, outdoor parties with live music and a giant inflatable Slip 'N Slide, Western parties with mechanical bulls, and even an annual party that lasts 24 straight hours. CMC students put all their creativity and smarts into planning completely imaginative, and sometimes wacky, parties—and the students love it."

The College Prowler Take On...
Nightlife

Claremont's student government (ASCMC) provides all of the nightlife most students need. Campus parties are the main events, and CMC kicks the weekend off right with a Thursday Night Club every week. Most weekend nights feature a big Five College Party with a fun theme like Smiley '80s, the Lei Party, or Revenge of the Nerds—people generally don costumes, although effort and creativity levels vary. Beer is served at the parties to students of age, but most student find the taps at the numerous pre- and post-parties much more liberal.

Having an active on-campus social life means that you're never far from helpful RAs in case you or a friend overdoes it, that you never have to deal with the hassle of a fake ID and figuring out which bars are safe, and that you'll never drink and drive. Students who are 21 will find a bevy of bars near campus, although it would be stretching it to call them college-oriented. There are tons of great happy hour specials in the area. Although there is nothing in walking distance (with the exception of the Press), most things are close enough to have someone pick you up with no trouble. Anyone interested in clubbing has to travel farther afield, and as long as you're driving, you might as well go into LA where you'll find some of the best (and most expensive) clubs in the country. While most college budgets don't support weekly clubbing trips to LA, the occasional night on Sunset Boulevard or in Brentwood is pretty attractive.

The College Prowler® Grade on

Nightlife: A

A high grade in Nightlife indicates that there are many bars and clubs in the area that are easily accessible and affordable. Other determining factors include the number of options for the under-21 crowd and the prevalence of house parties.

Greek Life

The Lowdown On...
Greek Life

Number of Fraternities:
0

Number of Sororities:
0

→

Students Speak Out On...
Greek Life

"Greek life is simply not needed in an environment like CMC. In fact, every weekend it feels like everyone is part of the same fraternity and sorority."

Q "We like to joke that CMC is really one big fraternity/ sorority. **We all party together and hang out together**. I would not say that people here are cliquish, for the most part. Dry activities and alternative lifestyles are supported, but on weekend nights, it can be challenging to have fun without alcohol."

Q "**There's no exclusivity** about anything in Claremont—if you see a party, just walk by, and you'll be welcome to join. This is good."

Q "As a devout prospie deciding to come here, I would have **expected the raucous party scene to be more difficult for religious students**—and even for non-religious lifestyle conservatives like I was at that time— than it actually is."

Q "Greek life is looked down upon on the 5Cs. **We don't need Greek life** to have parties, because we have various avenues through which parties can be thrown (primarily the social affairs committee). It's easy to get funding— each dorm has funds, ASCMC has funds, the executive board has funds, the SAC chair has funds, everyone has money—so sometimes clubs will throw parties."

Q "Dry activities are definitely easy to come by. There is a dry-affairs committee. Despite the lack of Greek life, **students still find time to party**."

Q "**Your dorm becomes your Greek life**. The dorms get together for meetings, throw parties, play sports together, and generally just hang out. The social life is completely inclusive."

Q "ASCMC puts a lot of work and money into the on-campus parties. Some parties like Screw Your Roommate and Monte Carlo are especially extravagant. Kegs are paid for by student funds, and so beer is technically free. **A lot of parties are theme parties**, which you can either participate in or not. The dance parties are fun with good music but because of Scripps College the female/male ratio usually is more favorable for the guys. The parties thrown by the other Five Colleges—like Mudd's Trick or Drink and Long Tall Glasses, or Pomona's Smiley '80s—can be really fun, too."

Q "Generally, dry activities take place on Fridays and consist of some **really good food and music**. They also offer drive-in movies and such."

Q "**The ASCMC (Student Government) parties are very Greek in nature**. They are themed, well organized, and well attended. The weekly Party Inform that is sent to all members of the student body makes sure all students are included."

Q "No one really cares about frats and sororities; I think the one frat that they have at Pomona is a group of lame guys who cant get laid any other way. **The social life is very non-exclusive**—anyone can go anywhere, hang out with anyone, and make friends. It's very low-pressure and lots of fun. And we have a whole dry-affairs committee which plans fun stuff without alcohol, so there're lots of options."

Q "**CMC is like one giant coed fraternity**. I love how inclusive all the parties are—there's an emphasis on having a good time rather than what club or house you belong to."

Q "You're pretty much **guaranteed a party every** Thursday night with TNC (Thursday Night Club), and every Saturday night, as well. Friday nights we try to throw parties, but sometimes people don't want to host them. Friday nights are off and on."

The College Prowler Take On...
Greek Life

Claremont McKenna College replaces a Greek system with an active and effective student government. When you put lots of smart econ and government majors together, you get a student government that is an independent corporation with a $250,000 annual budget whose only goal is to make life on campus fun. ASCMC supports every type of student activity, for example: paying for buses for a Vegas trip, subsidizing tickets for an LA Kings game, or reimbursing party hosts for kegs, cups and other expenses. ASCMC has the money and energy to make almost anything possible, but they don't hand it to students on a silver platter. On-campus and off-campus entertainment is student-motivated, meaning that while ASCMC will fund and help plan, the ideas come for the students.

Students can get involved with ASCMC in high level positions like president of the student body, or in less demanding roles as dorm presidents or senators. Every level of student government has an ample budget and plays a different role in student life. Senate, for example, has about 40 members and their budget includes the band fund, which gives them a say over who comes to perform at CMC. ASCMC is also responsible for the quality of student life beyond the borders of the College, since organizations and party planners from all over the Five Colleges come to ASCMC to get funding for 5C events on other campuses. CMC students don't miss the Greek system; ASCMC fully compensates for the parties and creates a more inclusive, all-around social life.

The College Prowler® Grade on

Greek Life: N/A

A high grade in Greek Life indicates that sororities and fraternities are not only present, but also active on campus. Other determining factors include the variety of houses available and the respect the Greek community receives from the rest of the campus.

Drug Scene

The Lowdown On...
Drug Scene

Most Prevalent Drugs on Campus:
Alcohol
Marijuana

Liquor-Related Referrals:
5

Liquor-Related Arrests:
1

Drug-Related Referrals:
5

Drug-Related Arrests:
3

→

Drug Counseling Programs

Alcoholics Anonymous

(909) 624-2712

Student Health Services

757 College Way

(909) 621-8222

Services: Emergency care, immunizations, regular appointments, women's health

Students Speak Out On...
Drug Scene

"Like anywhere, people smoke pot, but mainly, people here just drink. I've only heard of a few people who have done anything worse than marijuana."

Q "Beer and Facebook are predominant drugs of choice at CMC. That's not to say the campus is drug-free, but compared to the greener pastures just north at Pitzer College, **drugs play a relatively small role** in the social scene. Harder drugs are not completely absent from the campus, but are far from commonplace. A large majority of CMC's student body will likely go through their college career without using any harder drugs, and most of these will likely not even observe them being used. Adderall and other attention-enhancing drugs have been increasing in popularity come finals time, though more for academic reasons than recreation."

Q "I'm not sure; I know **marijuana is prevalent**."

Q "Like most college campuses, pot is pretty readily available, but harder drugs are fairly hard to come by. Not too many people smoke cigarettes. **Drugs are there if you want them**, but definitely not in your face if you don't."

Q "I believe there are drugs there for those who seek them, but if you do not want to take part, **there is no pressure** to do so."

Q "Drugs are as prevalent as you want them to be. There are kids who do them, and if you go looking, you can find them. However, **everyone is really chill**, and peer pressure is extremely low in relation to drugs and slightly higher in relation to drinking."

Q "Basically, there is alcohol and **pot if you look for it**."

Q "About as much pot as any other college. **Almost no hard drugs**, with the exception of cocaine, which was popular for a little while."

Q "**I haven't really seen any drugs** since I've been here, except alcohol, I suppose."

Q "**Drugs are not that prevalent** on CMC's campus, especially hard drugs."

Q "The drug scene? **Minor**—nothing really, besides marijuana."

Q "**I wouldn't know**. If I needed drugs, I would call my Pitzer friends."

Q "We're probably **tamer than most** colleges."

The College Prowler Take On...
Drug Scene

Alcohol is by far the most prevalent drug on campus. There is beer at most major parties, and although at the biggest parties there is generally a pretty secure carding system, the same cannot be said for smaller dorm parties. Students of legal age are allowed to consume alcohol in the dorms (except for Stark Hall), and most students do drink to some degree. For the most part, CMCers who choose to drink do so in a pretty responsible way, and the culture is such that people look out for one another.

Marijuana is by far the most prevalent controlled substance on the campus, but strict school policy keep users discreet. Students caught with marijuana by Camp Sec or residential advisors face serious consequences from the school, or in the worst case, from local law enforcement. Alcohol and marijuana are the only drugs that students risk coming into contact with incidentally. A few students do use more dangerous drugs like cocaine or ecstasy, but they are few and far between, and their use is well hidden. Most importantly, at CMC there isn't any peer pressure to do anything any student doesn't want to. Students are too concerned with their own lives and their own fun to meddle with other people's interests.

A-

The College Prowler® Grade on

Drug Scene: A-

A high grade in the Drug Scene indicates that drugs are not a noticeable part of campus life; drug use is not visible, and no pressure to use them seems to exist.

Campus Strictness

The Lowdown On...
Campus Strictness

What Are You Most Likely to Get Caught Doing on Campus?

- Breaking into the pool at night (Even if you avoid the motion sensor on the way in, it goes off when you get out!)
- Keeping couches outside your room in North Quad
- Parking in the wrong lot
- Plagiarism
- Stealing a Camp Sec golf cart

Students Speak Out On...
Campus Strictness

{ **"While CMC does have certain policies that are enforced, for the most part students are allowed to live life as they choose. I believe this allows the students to grow up faster and become a mature adult on their own."**

Q "**Campus rules are pretty lenient** for students who like to party, but most people realize that will only last as long as we keep being safe, responsible, and relatively clean. As soon as people start acting stupid and the administration feels like things are out of control, they'll clamp down."

Q "Recently, Camp Sec has been more strict. Comparatively, though (among all American colleges), **they're pretty lenient**."

Q "We are **pretty relaxed** about drugs and drinking. The administration knows it goes on and basically makes sure nothing gets out of control. As long as you aren't damaging anything or anyone, you will be left alone. So they're not very strict."

Q "Campus policies are **far more restrictive towards drug use than alcohol**. The informal College policy regarding alcohol is 'safety first.' This means we rarely, if ever, have binge drinking problems. Most students at CMC are out to have a good time, and the College provides a safe environment for students."

Q "**Camp Sec is super chill** compared to anywhere else. At most, they'll make you chug your open container if they see you walking around with it. They will call you out for smoking pot in public, but not if it's your room."

Q "Camp Sec is—how do I put this politically?—**respectful of my way of life**. And by that I mean it takes a lot to get them to hop out of their golf carts. They'd be there if I asked, though!"

Q "I'm not so sure about drugs. If you somehow got caught, **I'm sure the school would take some sort of action against you**. However, I doubt security goes out of its way to hunt down drug users."

Q "Because the only place to party on our campus is outside, **rules are less strict than most campuses**. As long as you are safe and responsible, you will stay out of trouble."

Q "Let's just say it **works out well**."

The College Prowler Take On...
Campus Strictness

Claremont McKenna College is very trusting of its students, so the unspoken general rule is: don't do anything stupid. CMC residential advisors are more like older siblings who are there to help you out; they provide stress counseling, help solve roommate issues, and when someone overdoes it at a party, they are concerned with getting help rather than figuring out whom to blame. They're also just good friends whose doors are always open. The school administration generally doesn't take a hard line when it comes to social issues, unless they strongly feel the event is harmful or offensive to some students. Camp Sec is truly a safety-oriented organization for CMC, not party poopers. Although they will occasionally shut down parties for noise complaints, you will often see them just standing harmlessly outside of a party, just in case something goes wrong.

There are a few areas where Claremont McKenna does take the rules very seriously. Plagiarism and cheating are completely unacceptable and will result in at least academic probation; it's not uncommon for first-time offenders to be suspended for a semester, depending on the severity of the offense. Claremont McKenna will also not tolerate any sort of hate crime—the school interprets the definition of hate crime very liberally to cover any type of writing, speech, or act that victimizes any group of people. The quickest way to get yourself in trouble at CMC is to scribble some 'joke' on a cultural awareness poster.

The College Prowler® Grade on

Campus Strictness: A

A high Campus Strictness grade implies an overall lenient atmosphere; police and RAs are fairly tolerant, and the administration's rules are flexible.

Parking

The Lowdown On...
Parking

Approximate Parking Permit Cost:
$40 per semester

Parking Services:
Five College Parking Services
251 E. 11th St.
(909) 621-8170

Freshmen Allowed to Park?
Yes

Student Parking Lot?
Yes, six areas: Bauer, North Quad, Marks, 6th and Mills, 6th across from the football field and the Student Apartment Complex (for residents only)

Common Parking Tickets:
No Parking Zone: $20
Failure to Register: $50
Fire Lane: $80
Handicapped Zone: $100

Parking Permits

Parking permits are really easy to acquire with a trip up the block to register with Camp Sec. There is no limit on the number of students who can apply.

Did You Know?

Best Places to Find a Parking Spot:
6th and Mills

Bauer

Good Luck Getting a Parking Spot Here:
North Quad Lot

South Quad Lot on Amherst

Students Speak Out On...
Parking

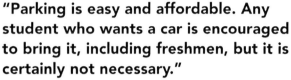

"Parking is easy and affordable. Any student who wants a car is encouraged to bring it, including freshmen, but it is certainly not necessary."

Q "We all complain if we have to walk five feet from our parking spot to our room. **Compared to anywhere else, our parking is heaven**."

Q "**Parking is easy**."

Q "It's easy to find parking, but **hard to find good parking**. The biggest lot that borders our campus belongs to Pomona, and they won't let us park there, so we have some big, nice, but inconvenient parking lots. You can always find a spot, but you might have to walk a bit."

Q "**It is very easy to find parking**. Yes, there are times when you will have to walk a little further than you would have liked, but unlike huge universities, 'a little further' is only a block."

Q "**Parking is never easy**, but you can always find a spot."

Q "Although some students complain about the parking, it is never impossible to find parking on campus. The issue with parking is that some dorms, most notably Mid Quad, do not have adequate parking in their vicinity. This is frustrating for students of those dorms, but there is **always parking available** in other lots if a student is willing to walk the extra distance (and since CMC's campus is so small, this distance is not excessive)."

Q "**It can sometimes be difficult to find parking** spots, but there are always options. You just might have to walk a little further than expected, but on a small campus it is not a big deal."

Q "Just about **everyone has a car**, so parking sucks, especially if you drive a truck or SUV."

Q "**Parking isn't bad**. It's a little hard sometimes to find a stall, so make friends with an RA who doesn't have a car, and take their staff parking pass; that way you can park anywhere."

The College Prowler Take On...
Parking

Because it takes less than 10 minutes to walk between any parking lot and any dorm, parking on campus is hardly an issue. There are two lots on the north side of campus and three on the south side, and there is enough parking in each to ensure that students can park on their side of campus. The school built a new lot recently, increasing the number of spots available to students. While you can't be assured a spot outside your door, you can always expect to be just a quick walk from home. Parking is pretty cheap, and freshmen are allowed to have cars on campus. About 40 percent of freshmen, and a bit over half of the total student body, have cars on campus.

Although you never need a car within the campuses, California is not particularly pedestrian-friendly, and having a car is useful. That doesn't mean that not having a car restricts students to campus; however, because there is never a lack of cars to get people to Target, LA, or the beach, and for most many major activities off campus the school rents a bus. Rides to the airport are always easy to get, and students who have a car can expect to give quite a few. CMC is so campus-centric that even students who have cars won't be using them to find things to do off campus on weekends. Any students thinking of bringing a car from outside of Southern California should understand that traffic is really is as bad as advertised and can be very stressful. Except for traffic, however, having a car at CMC couldn't be much easier.

The College Prowler® Grade on

Parking: A

A high grade in the Parking section indicates that parking is both available and affordable, and that parking enforcement isn't overly severe.

Transportation

The Lowdown On...
Transportation

Ways to Get Around Town:

On Campus
Walking, skateboarding, and biking (although campus is almost too small for that) are the best ways to get around. CMC also offers an occasional shuttle to local shopping centers.

Public Transportation

Foothill Transit
(800) 743-3463
www.foothilltransit.org

Metrolink
(800) 371-5465
www.metrolinktrains.com

Metropolitan Transit Authority
(800) 266-6883

Taxi Cabs

Yellow Cab of Claremont
(909) 621-0699

Car Rentals

Advantage
Local: (909) 390-3977
National: (800) 777-5500
www.arac.com

Alamo
Local: (909) 937-3600
National: (800) 462-5266
www.alamo.com

Avis
Local: (909) 390-1441
National: (800) 331-1212
www.avis.com

Budget
Local: (909) 937-6400
National: (800) 527-0700
www.budget.com

Dollar
Local: (866) 434-2226
National: (800) 800-4000
www.dollar.com

Enterprise
Local: (909) 624-5544
National: (800) 261-7331
www.enterprise.com

Hertz
Local: (909) 937-8877
National: (800) 654-3131
www.hertz.com

National
Local: (909) 937-7555
National: (800) 227-7368
www.nationalcar.com

Best Ways to Get Around Town

Bum a ride

Bike

Comfy flip-flops (rainbows are worth the price)

MetroLink to LA

Ways to Get Out of Town:

Airports

Ontario International
Airport (ONT)
(909) 937-2700
www.lawa.org/ont
Ontario International Airport is 10 miles and a 15-minute drive from Claremont McKenna.

Long Beach International
Airport (LGB)
(562) 570-2619
www.longbeach.gov/airport
Long Beach International is 42 miles and a 45-minute drive from Claremont McKenna.

Los Angeles International
Airport (LAX)
(310) 646-5252
www.lawa.org/lax
Los Angeles is 50 miles and at least an hour from Claremont McKenna.

Airlines Serving Ontario

Alaska Airlines
(800) 252-7522
www.alaskairlines.com

American Airlines
(800) 433-7300
www.americanairlines.com

Continental
(800) 523-3273
www.continental.com

Delta
(800) 221-1212
www.delta-air.com

JetBlue Airways
(800) 538-2583
www.jetblue.com

Southwest
(800) 435-9792
www.southwest.com

United
(800) 241-6522
www.united.com

U.S. Airways
(800) 428-4322
www.usairways.com

How to Get to the Airports

Distances in the Inland Empire are generally far, and cabs are prohibitively expensive, however SuperShuttle can be a good way to get to the airport; call (909) 467-9600. A shuttle ride costs $19 to Ontario International, $55 to Long Beach International, and $51 to Los Angeles International.

Greyhound

Pasadena Terminal
645 E. Walnut St.

(626) 792-5116

www.greyhound.com

The closest Greyhound Trailways Bus Terminal is located in Pasadena, 28 miles from Claremont McKenna. For schedule information call (800) 231-2222.

Amtrak

Claremont Station (CLM)
200 W. 1st St.

(800) 872-7245

www.amtrak.com

Amtrak offers very limited service from the train station in the Village, less than a mile from campus.

Travel Agents

Claremont Travel
325 Yale Ave.

(909) 621-3947

Students Speak Out On...
Transportation

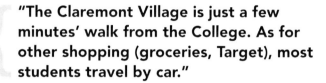

"The Claremont Village is just a few minutes' walk from the College. As for other shopping (groceries, Target), most students travel by car."

Q "For the love of God, fly into Ontario Airport. **Don't fly into LAX if it is the last airport on Earth**. No one will pick you up from LAX, and you'll have to live in a box outside the terminal for the rest of your life. Get it?"

Q "Is there public transportation? Really? Wow, **I had no idea**."

Q "If you want to get into LA, **the metro is 5 minutes away**. You can also take the bus, which is readily available."

Q "Public transportation in Southern California is a **horrific catastrophe** and should be avoided as much as possible."

Q "There is **definitely a benefit to having your own car**, but if you need to get somewhere, more often then not you will know people on campus with a car that will help you out."

Q "If you love the planet, take the Metrolink into LA, if you can find it. If you love yourself, drive. Actually, with traffic and all, **just don't go downtown** at all."

Q "Public transportation is available, but only to a limited extent. Students who come from areas with an extensive public transportation system will find that it is much more difficult to get around using public transportation around Claremont. Most students who do not have cars rely on friends with vehicles to go places. There are a few destinations of worth within walking distance (most notably the Village), but in general, **access to a friend's car (if not one's own) is almost necessary**."

Q "There **isn't really public transportation**, except a bus that comes, like, every two hours. However, most things are close by, and cars are usually pretty available."

Q "I have a car. For me, that definitely made life easier. However, **lots of people have cars**, so if you don't have one, it shouldn't really be a problem trying to find someone who will drive you wherever you need to go."

Q "**Mass transit is not an option**. You'll have better luck going from door to door begging for a ride."

Q "I've only used the Greyhound to go to Santa Barbara and San Diego. Strange experience. But **I recommend it**."

Q "There is no real public transportation. **There's the bus, but that's about it**."

The College Prowler Take On...
Transportation

Getting around Claremont McKenna's campus is easy, since it is only a 15-minute walk between the furthest points. Most people walk, and a lot of students skateboard. Bikes are common, too, although the short distances almost make them unnecessary. CMC is centrally located within the 5Cs, which means you are never more than 15 minutes from any point on any other campus. There is no shuttle to get around campus—it's not needed, and the campuses are limited almost entirely to foot traffic anyway. Getting around the local area is a little bit trickier without a car. There is some mass transit, but it isn't used much by students, and it can be difficult to figure out. To get into downtown LA, the Metrolink commuter train is pretty easy. Foothill Transit buses can be caught on Foothill Boulevard on the northern boarder of Harvey Mudd and can be used to get around the local area in Claremont, Upland, and Montclair.

Getting to Claremont McKenna isn't hard, since suburban LA is served by a number of airports. Given a choice, always choose Ontario International Airport, since it is easiest and most traffic-free. Long Beach International is okay, but it is small, and flights can be hard to find. As attractive and obvious as it may seem, avoid LAX at all costs. The traffic between Claremont and LAX is completely unpredictable but almost always horrible. Claremont isn't served by Greyhound or Amtrak, and it is probably more stress than it is worth to figure out how to take the bus or train.

The College Prowler® Grade on

Transportation: C

A high grade for Transportation indicates that campus buses, public buses, cabs, and rental cars are readily-available and affordable. Other determining factors include proximity to an airport and the necessity of transportation.

Weather

The Lowdown On...
Weather

Average Temperature:

Fall:	80 °F
Winter:	68 °F
Spring:	73 °F
Summer:	87 °F

Average Precipitation:

Fall:	0.74 in.
Winter:	3.37 in.
Spring:	1.47 in.
Summer:	0.06 in.

Students Speak Out On...
Weather

{ **"Don't bring anything too warm, but do bring some rain clothes and a good umbrella. T-shirts and jeans are always en vogue."**

Q "Probably one of the best parts about going to school in California is the weather. While your friends back east are trudging through snow to classes and social events, you'll be in shorts and flip-flops or in a bathing suit tanning by the pool! If you miss the snow, the good news is, we're only about **an hour away from some great skiing**."

Q "Even when it's warm during the day, **it can be chilly at night**."

Q "Flip-flops, flip-flops, flip-flops. You can get by with them all year. It can get really rainy, though. **Bring a pair of rain boots**. Skirts are great."

Q "Weather is usually warm, though **nights are colder than most people would think** for SoCal."

Q "Weather is usually very good. It can get cold at night, so light jackets and sweaters and sweatshirts are a must. You don't need a heavy coat, though, for sure. It's California weather, so **we wear skirts and shorts all year long**."

Q "You can almost always count on **73 degrees during the day and 55 degrees at night** during most of the year."

Q "**Weather is awesome**. Cold at night, hot in the day."

Q "It is very warm at the beginning and end of the school year, so warm-weather clothing is obviously a must. It is also highly recommended to bring cold-weather clothing, as it can get chilly, especially at night (overnight lows can be in the 30s during the winter). The most important piece of advice I can give regarding weather is to bring an umbrella! Many new students have the impression that no umbrella or raingear is needed in sunny Southern California. This is simply not true, and these students become soaked when we receive heavy rains around November. Although it does not rain often here, **it rains very hard when it finally does**!"

Q "Sunny. **The weather is always sunny**. It can get a little chilly at night, but overall, the weather is fantastic."

Q "Sunny Southern California. Don't worry about packing a parka—you will never wear it. **Do worry about finding the perfect swimsuit**—you'll need it when you skip class to lounge by the pool."

Q "The weather is **absolutely perfect**! It's SoCal!"

Q "Know this: it's really hot at the beginning of the school year. Nights get really cold during the winter. Other than that, the weather is **pretty sunny and mild**."

Q "The weather is awesome. It's pretty hot/warm up until October, sometimes later, and cools down a bit and gets kinda rainy until March, then it's **warm and pleasant** again after that. I've eaten lunch outside up until December, so it's very unpredictable."

Q "Our major weather excitement comes in the form of **massive brush fires** in the fall. We've had them two out of my three years thus far. Frankly, they are gorgeous at night on the ridgeline above us."

The College Prowler Take On...
Weather

Come on, admit it: you wouldn't be reading this book unless you were hoping for a little extra sunshine in your life for the next four years. Well, Southern California certainly won't disappoint. The California sun warms CMC pretty much year-round, and most of the time students spend outside of the classroom is outdoors. The first few weeks of the school year are pretty rough on the dorms without air-conditioning, but a trip to the pool is a quick fix for that. Hot days and warm nights persist into late October and sometime beyond, and it stays pleasantly warm during the day into December. There is often a hot spell for a week or two at the beginning of the second semester, but that soon gives way to February and March rain, along with the coolest daytime temperatures of the year. It doesn't rain much after March, and it begins to warm up around graduation time.

Pants and short-sleeve tops or tank tops work in the daytime for most of the school year, and people wear flip-flops year-round. Sweatshirts, sweaters, and light jackets are good for the winter and the cooler nights in the fall and spring, but students hardly ever need a heavy jacket. Bring rain gear—it will rain in the spring, but raincoats won't see the light of day most of the year. Earthquakes are a concern for some out-of-state students, and they do happen, but they are noticeable only in extremely extraordinary circumstances. Southern California weather is one stereotype you can believe; you'll want to hit the beach a lot.

The College Prowler® Grade on

Weather: A+

A high Weather grade designates that temperatures are mild and rarely reach extremes, that the campus tends to be sunny rather than rainy, and that weather is fairly consistent rather than unpredictable.

Report Card Summary

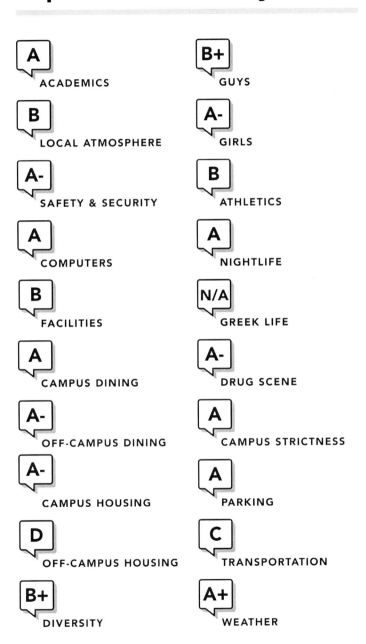

A — ACADEMICS

B — LOCAL ATMOSPHERE

A- — SAFETY & SECURITY

A — COMPUTERS

B — FACILITIES

A — CAMPUS DINING

A- — OFF-CAMPUS DINING

A- — CAMPUS HOUSING

D — OFF-CAMPUS HOUSING

B+ — DIVERSITY

B+ — GUYS

A- — GIRLS

B — ATHLETICS

A — NIGHTLIFE

N/A — GREEK LIFE

A- — DRUG SCENE

A — CAMPUS STRICTNESS

A — PARKING

C — TRANSPORTATION

A+ — WEATHER

Overall Experience

Students Speak Out On...
Overall Experience

"It's so much fun; everyone is very friendly, and I absolutely love it here. The only bad thing is all the requirements; I feel like I won't be able to take fun classes like art that don't have much to do with my major."

Q "I am so glad I came here. At a bigger school, I would be competing for opportunities that, at CMC, are here for the taking. **It's incredibly easy to get involved**, get jobs, and make friends. I feel so successful here, and I know that if I didn't, it would be easy to get help."

Q "**I've loved CMC since I first visited**, and that love has only gotten stronger. I would share a personal memory, but I can't think of anything legal at the moment."

Q "Most people who go to CMC and don't like it just leave (the usual complaints are the narrow educational focus and that it's not a traditional liberal arts school). Thus, you have a remainder that is devoted to CMC. My least favorite part is the lack of cable television on campus (but that is changing). My favorite part is the Athenaeum and brunch on the weekends. There is no college like CMC anywhere else. **It is amazing how well we are taken care of and cared for**. One must appreciate it now because the real world is beginning to seem like a pretty scary place compared to the paradise that is CMC."

Q "My favorite part is also my least favorite part of the campus: the smallness. When I think of CMC, I think of the intimate access to the professors, the late-night debates, and the all around wholesomeness and awesomeness of the student body. Students are here to learn, have fun, and contribute. It makes for **a great intellectual and social atmosphere**."

Q "**It can feel small at times**, but if that happens, I just go visit friends at Pomona or Scripps. I am currently class president, and that is something I never would have done in high school, or at a bigger school. I just wouldn't have felt confident enough or ambitious enough. I feel really fulfilled on academic, personal, and professional levels here, and I hope that anyone who is thinking about coming here knows that your experience at college is what you choose to make it, but at CMC it feels easier to make it happen."

Q "Here students can truly be themselves and **live whatever lifestyle they choose**."

Q "**My experience has been incredible**, and I would do it again in a second. My favorite parts have been the people, and my least favorite parts have been the finals—however, I'm pretty sure those are unavoidable."

Q "I would come here all over again. Least favorite parts: Village gets repetitive, I want more places to walk. **I love the people**. Sometimes it can be so small in terms of the number of people, but when that happens, go eat at Harvey Mudd; you'll definitely see people you've never met!"

Q "I wasn't really sure about where I wanted to go to college and ended up sort of falling into CMC because the athletic department recruits really well. Luckily, CMC ended up being the most perfect fit for me. I really like going to a small school. The small school experience is not for everyone, but it's definitely right for me. I like the intimacy of the campus. I like rolling out of bed two minutes before class starts and being on time because things are just that close. I like that I've been able to form real personal connections with my teachers and the large majority of my class. There are **so many amazing resources and opportunities** offered by CMC."

Q "I went with a professor and small group of students to Korea last summer, and through my professor's connections was able to meet with the former Prime Minister of Korea, the ambassador to the UN and EU, and other amazing political figures. The Career Services Center and Community Service Office are staffed by some really amazing people who are **truly dedicated to helping students**. CMC encourages and facilitates active involvement on campus, which is really what I was looking for in a college."

Q "If I could do it all again, I would still pick CMC. **It's a wonderful place** with professors and staff who really care about the students, and overall, all they're trying to do is keep the kids happy and having fun. The best thing about CMC is the quality of the education I'm getting, the feeling that we're a community, not a school, and that everyone really cares about what happens to each individual student."

The College Prowler Take On...
Overall Experience

Claremont McKenna College fits in well with its easygoing Southern California surroundings. The quality of life is great and day-to-day living is easy, despite the academic challenges presented by classes. The climate is friendly, the dorms are nice, and most of the things students really need are on campus. The surrounding area provides a ton of entertainment possibilities for all types of people. While CMCers don't leave learning and in-class discussions at the door, they aren't bookworms or indoor intellectuals with one-track minds. Academics is mixed into daily life and woven into each individual's interests. Classes try to maintain a balance between intellectualism and pragmatism. The Five College Consortium makes available huge numbers of classes, far more than the typical 1,000-student school.

The on-campus social life is very active and creative. Students who come to CMC looking for an active bar and club scene will likely be disappointed, but those who look to campus as an entertainment source will find their needs met. Sometimes, the social scene seems drinking-oriented, but there are many options for non-drinkers and plenty of reasons to go to parties besides the keg. By far, the things that make CMC unique are the living, breathing student bodies that learn and play on campus. CMC's small student body gathers together a huge array of interests and personality types, so a general characterization is impossible, but a few generalizations are safe: everyone is intelligent and interested in learning, but no one is interested solely in learning; the students like to have fun in their own ways and are mostly unconcerned with how other people enjoy themselves; CMCers are opinionated but respectful of other students' opinions and can talk about them in an intellectual way. The student body is more diverse in interests and experience than it is in color and ethnicity, but the academic program and social agenda at CMC make it possible for a lot of different people to find their niche and be happy. Above all else, students should feel happy at their college!

The Inside Scoop

The Lowdown On...
The Inside Scoop

CMC Slang:

Know the slang, know the school. The following is a list of things you really need to know before coming to CMC. The more of these words you know, the better off you'll be.

5Cs – The Five College Consortium: Claremont McKenna, Pitzer, Scripps, Harvey Mudd, and Pomona.

The Ath – The Athenaeum, the nice dining room where we host our speaker series and eat delicious food.

The Buf – The Buffalo Inn; has good happy hour deals.

Camp Sec – Campus security force.

GE – General Education; basic requirement classes you need to take to graduate.

Green Beach – The grassy spot between Green dorm and Parents field, named a beach because we're too lazy to actually go to a real beach.

Informs – The e-mail information messages sent to students daily.

The Lei – Shady strip club on foothill—funniest signs ever.

Mix Bowl – Local fast food Thai place open late. Avoid the Hotdog Pad Thai.

Parents – The big grassy field to play on between Green and the Towers.

Pods – The little lounge buildings attached to the North Quad dorms with huge rooms on top.

Ponding – Getting thrown in the fountain on your birthday (and sometimes for no reason at all).

Poppa – The main computer lab on campus. Actually named after an alumnus, and not because it's the big daddy lab.

Prospie – A visiting high school student, so, you.

Round Table – Pizza place open late. Kinda like cheesy cardboard.

RTA – Resident Technology Assistant, the person who can solve all your computer troubles.

South Park – The computer lab in South Quad in the Stark Dorm.

Story House – The facilities office, responsible for keeping the campus looking amazing 24/7.

The Towers – Auen, Fawcett and Stark, the South Quad seven story dorms.

The Village – The little four block shopping area a few minutes away with great restaurants and cool local clothing boutiques.

Things I Wish I Knew Before Coming to CMC

- Go on a WOA! trip (Wilderness Orientation Adventure).

- CMC's Orientation is about as much fun as any human being can have.

- ASCMC, the student government, buys your alcohol.

- Fly into Ontario Airport; avoid LAX!

- CMC is about more than economics and government.

Tips to Succeed at CMC

• Go to all the tech orientation sessions.

• Go to office hours!

• Go to your local new students party.

• Make your RTA your best friend.

• If you don't own a pair or flip flops, get some Reefs or Rainbows.

• For the love of all things holy, go abroad!

• Read the informs, or you'll have no idea what's up.

• Go to tutoring and use the Writing Center.

CMC Urban Legends

• Robin Williams was expelled after just a semester for crashing a golf cart into the dining hall.

• Before building the towers, CMC bought the town of Claremont a fire truck tall enough to reach the top so that the school could get their building plans approved.

• Abercrombie & Fitch is the only interview the Career Services will tell you not to dress up for.

School Spirit

CMCers love CMC, but it isn't school spirit in the traditional sense. People don't turn out to every football game to root for the Stags (although we'll always come out to talk trash to Pomona), but the school spirit manifests itself mainly through the social life. CMCers are always looking for a new, creative, over-the-top, indulgent way to all have fun together. School spirit is best seen in big afternoon barbeques with Slip 'N Slides down Green Beach, or in the wee hours of the marathon 24-hour party, or during an intense game of IM inner tube water polo.

Traditions

Monte Carlo

For Homecoming each year, ASCMC turns the dining hall into a giant casino with blackjack, poker, and roulette. Outside there is a hardwood dance floor where couples can swing dance to big band music all night long. Chips won in the casino can be traded in for raffle tickets with two tickets to Hawaii as the top prize.

Finding a Job or Internship

The Lowdown On...
Finding a Job or Internship

Career Center:

Career Services Center
Claremont McKenna College
Heggblade Center
850 Columbia Ave.

(909) 607-7038

csc.claremontmckenna.edu

Grads Entering the Job Market:

Within 6 Months: 62%
Within 1 Year: N/A
Within 2 Years: N/A

Services Available:

Access to Internet job databases

Career counseling

Community service and volunteering workshops

Cover letter reviews

Employer presentations

Graduate school presentations

Interviewing workshops

Job search strategies

Networking workshops

Personality testing

Resume workshops

Firms That Most Frequently Hire Grads

Accenture, Access Industries, AM Productions & Management, Amazon. com, AmeriCorps - Turning the Page, Bear Stearns & Co. , Behavioral Neurogenetics Research Center at Stanford University, BIA (Bathish Insurance Agency), Boeing, Brown McCarroll, Burnside and Associates, California State Capitol Fellowships, Cambridge Associates, Deloitte Consulting, Educational Services International, Enterprise Advertising, Enterprise Rent-a-Car, Envision Telephony, Fairmont Designs, Ferguson Enterprises, Financial Network - ING Advisors, Flir Systems, Inc, FTI Consulting, Fulcrum Financial Inquiry, Goldman Sachs, JET Program, Johnson & Johnson Pharmaceutical Research & Development, JPL, JP Morgan Private Bank, Kenmar Research Institute, Kohgakusha co. ltd, KPMG, Lake Partners Strategy Consultants, Lehman Brothers, Los Angeles County Arts Commission, Lt. Governor Campaign in Boston, Mark IV Capital, Macy's, Marsh & McLennan, Martinsville Daily, Steven Myers and Associates, National Economic Research Associates, National Institutes of Health, Navigant Consulting, Net Impact, New Line Cinema, Northern Trust Bank, Peace Corps, PepsiCo, Peter Miller Details, Pfizer, PricewaterhouseCoopers, Planned Parenthood of MN, SD & ND, Prager, Sealy & Co. , PricewaterhouseCoopers, Prindle, Decker & Amaro, Robert Charles Lesser Co, RSM Equico, Target Corporation, Teach for America, The Abernathy MacGregor Group, The Concord Group, The Fund for Public Interest Research, The Jewish Community Relations Council, The Nova Group, The Posse Foundation, Towers Perrin, Troon Golf, Trust Company of the West Tucker Alan, UC San Diego, UCLA - Digestive Disease Research Lab, Unified Consulting, U. S. Army, U. S. Department of Agriculture- Forest Service, US Department of Justice - Antitrust Division, U. S. Department of State, Villanova Prep High School, Western Asset Management, Wexler and Walker Public Policy Associates, Wright Capital Partners - Private Equity Group, ZS Associates, The White House, Washington DC

Advice

CMC's Career Services Center is available to students looking for post graduate work, summer internships, or just general career advice. Most students would agree that the office is best at helping econ and accounting majors find jobs, but that's partly due to the strong recruitment programs in place at most investment banks, consulting firms, and accounting firms. Over 100 firms visit CMC to recruit, including Teach For America, advertising and entertainment agencies, and political organizations. Around a quarter of every graduating class goes directly to graduate school—mostly law school—so the Career Service Center also provides support for grad school applications.

Firms also come to campus to recruit for summer internships, although the process is less organized. The Center can connect students with alumni in the field and location they wish to work. CMC's alumni network is very supportive, and this can be a great way to find a job. Many students aren't completely satisfied with the Career Services Center and find they have to do a lot of work on their own, but the Center does offer a helpful variety of support services.

Some further points to remember:

- Go into the Career Services Center a little earlier in your college life than you think you might need to. Talking to the counselors can make everything seem a little less confusing.
- Go to on-campus events with Alumni and Ath talks that interest you and use the opportunity to network.
- Pay attention to your Informs for internship opportunities.
- The Kravis Leadership Institute gives grants to students who work unpaid internships at not-for-profit organizations both domestically and internationally.
- The Mentor Café, the alumni mentorship program, can be a great way to talk to someone who can help you figure out what types of careers might suit you and help you figure out how to get the job you want.

Average Salary Information

About two thirds of each graduating class heads directly into the workforce; these are 2005 average reported salaries for those students, separated by their field or industry.

Accounting	$45,611
Business	$37,744
Consulting	$51,026
Education	$31,218
Financial Services	$59,500
Investment Banking	$55,357
Government/Law	$32,260
Medical/Health	$25,000
Science & Tech	$48,220
Other	$28,833

Alumni

The Lowdown On...
Alumni

Web Site:
www.claremontmckenna.edu/ alumnigateway

Office:
Office of Alumni Relations
Claremont McKenna College
400 N. Claremont Blvd.
(909) 621-8097

Alumni Publications:
CMC Magazine reports on the successes of alumni and current students, and is published quarterly.

Services Available:
Alumni directory

CMC merchandise

International travel-oriented reunions

Membership to CMCAA (Claremont's Alumni Association)

Webcasts of Athenaeum events

Alumni Giving Rate:
49%

Did You Know?

Famous CMC Alumni:

Raymond Remy (Class of 1959) – Former Deputy Mayor of Los Angeles

Robert Nakasone (Class of 1969) – Former CWO of Toys 'R' Us

Karen Rosenfelt (Class of 1980) – Producer and former president of Paramount Pictures

Peter Thum (Class of 1990) – Founder of Ethos Water

Robin Williams (Did not graduate) – Actor, comedian

Student Organizations

5 College Chocolate Club

5C Activities Directors

5C Eco Club

5C Lindy Hop Club

After School Special

Animotion

Archery Club

Benjamin Franklin Society

Black Student Union

Bottom Line Theatre

Chess Club

Chiapas Support Committee

CIVITAS

Claremont Accounting Association

Claremont Braineaters Men's Ultimate Frisbee

Claremont Circle K

Claremont Colleges Badminton Club

Claremont Colleges Ballroom Dance Company

Claremont Colleges Cycling Club

Claremont Colleges Mariachi

Claremont Colleges Rowing Club

Claremont Colleges Triathlon Club

Claremont Colleges Women's Rugby Football Team

Claremont Entrepreneurial Society

Claremont Field Hockey

Claremont Historical Society

Claremont Hockey Club

Claremont International Relations Society

Claremont Political Action Network

Claremont Political Journal

Claremont Portside – Claremont's liberal political journal

Claremont Republicans

Claremont Shades

CMC Magazine – Claremont Student Newsmagazine

Claremont Surf Club

Climbing Team

CMC Korean Club

CMC Moonlight Ultimate Frisbee

CMS Cheer

Community Connections

CSAFE

Democrats of the Claremont Colleges

EKTA

Emergency Exit Productions

Empowered Black Women

Empowered Latinos/as in Action

Felons Softball Club

Figure Drawing Club

Food for Thought

Frank Lloyd Wright Society

Grupo de Capoeira Claremont

Habitat for Humanity

Hamagshimim

Hillel Knesset

Hui Laulea

International Club

InterVarsity Christian Fellowship

INVE$T

Italian Club

Itihad

Jewish Student Union

Joint Science Premed Club

Juggling Club – They juggle stuff

Korean American Student Association

KSPC

Libertarians of the Claremont Colleges

Male Dissent

March of Dimes

Men's Lacrosse

Men's Rugby

Mixed Martial Arts Club

Muslim Students Association

On the Loose

Pan-African Student Association

Passwords – Literary review magazine

Pathfinder Christian Fellowship

Peace and Justice Coalition

Pomona Valley Low-Income Services

Populus Christi

PP Hip-Hop Dance Team

PP Men's Club Volleyball

Pre-Law Society

QQAMP

Queer Resource Center

Questioning and Allied Mentorship Program

Really Ambitious Filmmaking Team

Religious Appreciation Group

The Re-View

Skateboarding Club

Ski/Snowboard Club

Society of Undergraduate Mathematicians

Stay Wild

Straight But Not Narrow

Student AIDS Awareness Committee

Student Investment Fund

Students for the Bernard Field Station

Studio 47

Taiko Club

Taiwanese Student Association

Tau Delta

The Class

TRANScend

Under the Lights

United Students Against Sweatshops

VOX – Planned Parenthood group

Whitewater Kayaking Club

Winston Churchill Women's Forum

Without a Box

Women's Ultimate Frisbee

The Best
& Worst

The Ten BEST Things About CMC

1	The Athenaeum
2	The professors
3	Parties like Monte Carlo, Professor Elliot's Singing Parties, and the Toga Party
4	Small, intimate classes
5	January by the pool
6	WOA! trips
7	Room cleaning
8	Being able to leave your door unlocked 24/7
9	IM inner tube water polo
10	Great food on and off campus

The Ten **WORST** Things About CMC

1 General education requirements

2 Proximity to Pomona

3 The invisible administration (except Dean Huang)

4 Small size

5 Distance from the beach

6 The utilitarian campus

7 Story House is OCD about furniture outside

8 Rainy season

9 Lack of a real student center

10 The "fight" song

Visiting

The Lowdown On...
Visiting

Hotel Information:

Claremont:

The Claremont Inn
555 Foothill Blvd.
(800) 854-5733
Distance from Campus: Less than a mile
Price Range: $69–$129

Upland:

Best Western Mountain View Inn & Suites
1191 East Foothill Blvd.
(909) 949-4800
Distance from Campus: 5 miles
Price Range: $90–$120

Pomona:

Sheraton Suites Fairplex
601 West McKinley Ave.
(909) 622-2220
Distance from Campus:
4.5 miles
Price Range: $129–$184

Shilo Inn Hotel
3200 Temple Ave.
(909) 598-0073
www.shiloinns.com/California/
pomona_hotel.html
Distance from Campus: 9 miles
Price Range: $100–$115

Shilo Inn Suites Hotel
3101 Temple Ave.
(909) 598-7666
www.shiloinns.com/California/
pomona_hilltop.html
Distance from Campus: 9 miles
Price Range: $135–$165

Ontario:

AmeriSuites Hotel – Ontario Airport
4760 E. Mills Circle
(909) 980-2200
Distance from Campus:
10 miles
Price Range: $90–$130

Ayers Suites – Ontario Mills
4370 Mills Circle
(909) 481-0703
www.ayreshotels.com/
ontariomills/index.asp
Distance from Campus: 10
miles
Price Range: $120–$150

Best Western – Ontario Airport
209 N. Vineyard Ave.
(909) 937-6800
Distance from Campus:
10 miles
Price Range: $75–$90

DoubleTree Hotel – Ontario Airport
222 North Vineyard Ave.
(909) 937-0900
Distance from Campus:
10 miles
Price Range: $140–$375

Country Side Suites – Ontario Airport
204 N. Vineyard Ave.
(909) 937-9700
www.ayreshotels.com/ontario/
index.asp
Distance from Campus:
10 miles
Price Range: $90–$110

Hilton – Ontario Airport

700 N. Haven Ave.

(909) 980-0400

Distance from Campus:
10 miles

Price Range: $125–$175

Marriott Fairfield Inn

3201 E. Centrelake Dr.

(909) 390-9835

Distance from Campus:
10 miles

Price Range: $90–$110

Marriott – Ontario Airport

2200 E. Holt Blvd.

(909) 975-5000

*http://marriott.com/property/
propertypage/ONTCA*

Distance from Campus
10 miles

Price Range: $150–$210

Marriott Residence Inn – Ontario Airport

2025 Convention Center Way

(909) 937-6788

*http://marriott.com/property/
propertypage/ONTVY*

Distance from Campus:
10 miles

Price Range: $150–$170

Sheraton – Ontario Airport Hotel

429 N. Vineyard Ave.

(909) 937-8000

Distance from Campus:
10 miles

Price Range: $115–$150

Covina:

Embassy Suites Hotel Los Angeles Covina/I-10

1211 E. Garvey St.

(626) 915-3441

Distance from Campus:
10 miles

Price Range: $100–$150

Schedule a Group Information Session or Interview

Interviews are done by appointment only. Monday–Friday 9, 10 and 11 a.m. and 1:30, 2:30, 3:30 p.m. Limited Saturday appointments are available. Interviews for high school seniors and transfer only and are offered between early summer and mid December. Information sessions are conducted at 9 a.m. and 1:30 p.m. on weekdays. Call (909) 621-8088 to schedule an interview or information session.

Take a Virtual Tour of Campus

www.claremontmckenna.edu/about/tour/

Campus Tours

Tours are given throughout the school year on weekdays at 10 and 11 a.m. and 2:30 and 3:30 p.m. Saturday tours are given September to December and in April and May at 10 a.m. Summer tours are given at 10 a.m. and 2:30 p.m. on weekdays. Appointments are recommended but not required. Call (909) 621-8088 to schedule a tour.

Overnight Visits

Overnight visits are a great way to get to know the student body a better and spend a fun night away from home. Overnight stays are especially useful for anyone who is applying to more than one of the five colleges and wants to better understand the differences between schools.

Visits can be scheduled at almost any time when school is in session except fall break, thanksgiving, spring break and finals weeks. Overnight visits must be scheduled two weeks in advance, so call ahead to check availability and make an appointment. The phone number is (909) 621-8088.

CMC also runs several on campus day admissions events in the fall (September and October), and overnight visits can be scheduled in conjunction with these days for students coming from a distance. Check the Web site (*www.claremontmckenna. edu/prospectives*) or watch the official mailing for exact dates.

Directions to Campus

Driving from the North

- Take the I-15 South to the CA-210 Westbound to Pasadena. Stay on I-210 West (towards Pasadena) until you reach the Towne Avenue exit.

- Turn left off the exit. You will be on Towne; continue south for about one mile until you reach Foothill Boulevard.

- Turn left on Foothill Boulevard. Continue east on Foothill for about one mile and turn right onto Dartmouth Avenue.

- Continue south on Dartmouth for three blocks to 10th Street and turn left.

- Follow 10th Street to Columbia and turn right. The Admission Office (890 Columbia Avenue) will be on your left just past 9th Street.

Driving from the South

- Take the CA-57 North to the I-10 Eastbound. Stay on the I-10 East (toward San Bernardino) until you reach the Indian Hill/Claremont exit.

- Turn left (north) off the exit. You will be on Indian Hill; continue north on Indian Hill for about 1.5 miles until you reach 10th Street.

- Turn right on 10th Street and follow it until it ends on Columbia.

- Turn right (south) on Columbia; the Admissions Office (890 Columbia) will be on your left just past 9th Street.

Or . . .

- Take the I-15 North to the I-10. Stay on I-10 West (toward Los Angeles) until you reach the Indian Hill/Claremont exit.

- Turn right (north) off the exit. You will be on Indian Hill; continue north on Indian Hill for about 1.5 miles until you reach 10th Street.

- Turn right on 10th Street and follow it until it ends on Columbia.

- Turn right (south) on Columbia; the Admissions Office (890 Columbia) will be on your left just past 9th Street.

Driving from the East

- Stay on I-10 West (toward Los Angeles) until you reach the Indian Hill/Claremont exit.

- Turn right (north) off the exit. You will be on Indian Hill; continue north on Indian Hill for about 1.5 miles until you reach 10th Street.

- Turn right on 10th Street and follow it until it ends on Columbia.

- Turn right (south) on Columbia; the Admissions Office (890 Columbia) will be on your left just past 9th Street.

Or . . .

- Stay on I-210 West (towards Pasadena) until you reach the Towne Avenue exit.

- Turn left off the exit. You will be on Towne; continue south for about one mile until you reach Foothill Boulevard.

- Turn left on Foothill Boulevard.

- Continue east on Foothill for about one mile and turn right onto Dartmouth Avenue.

- Continue south on Dartmouth for three blocks to 10th Street and turn left.

- Follow 10th Street to Columbia and turn right. The Admissions Office (890 Columbia Avenue) will be on your left just past 9th Street.

Driving from the West

- Stay on the I-10 East (toward San Bernardino) until you reach the Indian Hill/Claremont exit.

- Turn left (north) off the exit. You will be on Indian Hill; continue north on Indian Hill for about 1.5 miles until you reach 10th Street.

- Turn right on 10th Street and follow it until it ends on Columbia.

- Turn right (south) on Columbia; the Admission Office (890 Columbia) will be on your left just past 9th Street.

Or . . . (Driving from the West, continued)

- Stay on the I-210 East (towards San Bernardino) until you reach the Towne Avenue exit.

- Turn right off the exit. You will be on Towne; continue south for about one mile until you reach Foothill Boulevard.

- Turn left on Foothill Boulevard. Continue east on Foothill for about one mile and turn right onto Dartmouth Avenue.

- Continue south on Dartmouth for three blocks to 10th Street and turn left.

- Follow 10th Street to Columbia and turn right. The Admission Office (890 Columbia Avenue) will be on your left just past 9th Street.

Words to Know

Academic Probation – A suspension imposed on a student if he or she fails to keep up with the school's minimum academic requirements. Those unable to improve their grades after receiving this warning can face dismissal.

Beer Pong/Beirut – A drinking game involving cups of beer arranged in a pyramid shape on each side of a table. The goal is to get a ping pong ball into one of the opponent's cups by throwing the ball or hitting it with a paddle. If the ball lands in a cup, the opponent is required to drink the beer.

Bid – An invitation from a fraternity or sorority to 'pledge' (join) that specific house.

Blue-Light Phone – Brightly-colored phone posts with a blue light bulb on top. These phones exist for security purposes and are located at various outside locations around most campuses. In an emergency, a student can pick up one of these phones (free of charge) to connect with campus police or a security escort.

Campus Police – Police who are specifically assigned to a given institution. Campus police are typically not regular city officers; they are employed by the university in a full-time capacity.

Club Sports – A level of sports that falls somewhere between varsity and intramural. If a student is unable to commit to a varsity team but has a lot of passion for athletics, a club sport could be a better, less intense option. Even less demanding, intramural (IM) sports often involve no traveling and considerably less time.

Cocaine – An illegal drug. Also known as "coke" or "blow," cocaine often resembles a white crystalline or powdery substance. It is highly addictive and dangerous.

Common Application – An application with which students can apply to multiple schools.

Course Registration – The period of official class selection for the upcoming quarter or semester. Prior to registration, it is best to prepare several back-up courses in case a particular class becomes full. If a course is full, students can place themselves on the waitlist, although this still does not guarantee entry.

Division Athletics – Athletic classifications range from Division I to Division III. Division IA is the most competitive, while Division III is considered to be the least competitive.

Dorm – A dorm (or dormitory) is an on-campus housing facility. Dorms can provide a range of options from suite-style rooms to more communal options that include shared bathrooms. Most first-year students live in dorms. Some upperclassmen who wish to stay on campus also choose this option.

Early Action – An application option with which a student can apply to a school and receive an early acceptance response without a binding commitment. This system is becoming less and less available.

Early Decision – An application option that students should use only if they are certain they plan to attend the school in question. If a student applies using the early decision option and is admitted, he or she is required and bound to attend that university. Admission rates are usually higher among students who apply through early decision, as the student is clearly indicating that the school is his or her first choice.

Ecstasy – An illegal drug. Also known as "E" or "X," ecstasy looks like a pill and most resembles an aspirin. Considered a party drug, ecstasy is very dangerous and can be deadly.

Ethernet – An extremely fast Internet connection available in most university-owned residence halls. To use an Ethernet connection properly, a student will need a network card and cable for his or her computer.

Fake ID – A counterfeit identification card that contains false information. Most commonly, students get fake IDs with altered birthdates so that they appear to be older than 21 (and therefore of legal drinking age). Even though it is illegal, many college students have fake IDs in hopes of purchasing alcohol or getting into bars.

Frosh – Slang for "freshman" or "freshmen."

Hazing – Initiation rituals administered by some fraternities or sororities as part of the pledging process. Many universities have outlawed hazing due to its degrading, and sometimes dangerous, nature.

Intramurals (IMs) – A popular, and usually free, sport league in which students create teams and compete against one another. These sports vary in competitiveness and can include a range of activities—everything from billiards to water polo. IM sports are a great way to meet people with similar interests.

Keg – Officially called a half-barrel, a keg contains roughly 200 12-ounce servings of beer.

LSD – An illegal drug, also known as acid, this hallucinogenic drug most commonly resembles a tab of paper.

Marijuana – An illegal drug, also known as weed or pot; along with alcohol, marijuana is one of the most commonly-found drugs on campuses across the country.

Major –The focal point of a student's college studies; a specific topic that is studied for a degree. Examples of majors include physics, English, history, computer science, economics, business, and music. Many students decide on a specific major before arriving on campus, while others are simply "undecided" until declaring a major. Those who are extremely interested in two areas can also choose to double major.

Meal Block – The equivalent of one meal. Students on a meal plan usually receive a fixed number of meals per week. Each meal, or "block," can be redeemed at the school's dining facilities in place of cash. Often, a student's weekly allotment of meal blocks will be forfeited if not used.

Minor – An additional focal point in a student's education. Often serving as a complement or addition to a student's main area of focus, a minor has fewer requirements and prerequisites to fulfill than a major. Minors are not required for graduation from most schools; however some students who want to explore many different interests choose to pursue both a major and a minor.

Mushrooms – An illegal drug. Also known as "'shrooms," this drug resembles regular mushrooms but is extremely hallucinogenic.

Off-Campus Housing – Housing from a particular landlord or rental group that is not affiliated with the university. Depending on the college, off-campus housing can range from extremely popular to non-existent. Students who choose to live off campus are typically given more freedom, but they also have to deal with possible subletting scenarios, furniture, bills, and other issues. In addition to these factors, rental prices and distance often affect a student's decision to move off campus.

Office Hours – Time that teachers set aside for students who have questions about coursework. Office hours are a good forum for students to go over any problems and to show interest in the subject material.

Pledging – The early phase of joining a fraternity or sorority, pledging takes place after a student has gone through rush and received a bid. Pledging usually lasts between one and two semesters. Once the pledging period is complete and a particular student has done everything that is required to become a member, that student is considered a brother or sister. If a fraternity or a sorority would decide to "haze" a group of students, this initiation would take place during the pledging period.

Private Institution – A school that does not use tax revenue to subsidize education costs. Private schools typically cost more than public schools and are usually smaller.

Prof – Slang for "professor."

Public Institution – A school that uses tax revenue to subsidize education costs. Public schools are often a good value for in-state residents and tend to be larger than most private colleges.

Quarter System (or Trimester System) – A type of academic calendar system. In this setup, students take classes for three academic periods. The first quarter usually starts in late September or early October and concludes right before Christmas. The second quarter usually starts around early to mid–January and finishes up around March or April. The last academic quarter, or "third quarter," usually starts in late March or early April and finishes up in late May or Mid-June. The fourth quarter is summer. The major difference between the quarter system and semester system is that students take more, less comprehensive courses under the quarter calendar.

RA (Resident Assistant) – A student leader who is assigned to a particular floor in a dormitory in order to help to the other students who live there. An RA's duties include ensuring student safety and providing assistance wherever possible.

Recitation – An extension of a specific course; a review session. Some classes, particularly large lectures, are supplemented with mandatory recitation sessions that provide a relatively personal class setting.

Rolling Admissions – A form of admissions. Most commonly found at public institutions, schools with this type of policy continue to accept students throughout the year until their class sizes are met. For example, some schools begin accepting students as early as December and will continue to do so until April or May.

Room and Board – This figure is typically the combined cost of a university-owned room and a meal plan.

Room Draw/Housing Lottery – A common way to pick on-campus room assignments for the following year. If a student decides to remain in university-owned housing, he or she is assigned a unique number that, along with seniority, is used to determine his or her housing for the next year.

Rush – The period in which students can meet the brothers and sisters of a particular chapter and find out if a given fraternity or sorority is right for them. Rushing a fraternity or a sorority is not a requirement at any school. The goal of rush is to give students who are serious about pledging a feel for what to expect.

Semester System – The most common type of academic calendar system at college campuses. This setup typically includes two semesters in a given school year. The fall semester starts around the end of August or early September and concludes before winter vacation. The spring semester usually starts in mid-January and ends in late April or May.

Student Center/Rec Center/Student Union – A common area on campus that often contains study areas, recreation facilities, and eateries. This building is often a good place to meet up with fellow students; depending on the school, the student center can have a huge role or a non-existent role in campus life.

Student ID – A university-issued photo ID that serves as a student's key to school-related functions. Some schools require students to show these cards in order to get into dorms, libraries, cafeterias, and other facilities. In addition to storing meal plan information, in some cases, a student ID can actually work as a debit card and allow students to purchase things from bookstores or local shops.

Suite – A type of dorm room. Unlike dorms that feature communal bathrooms shared by the entire floor, suites offer bathrooms shared only among the suite. Suite-style dorm rooms can house anywhere from two to ten students.

TA (Teacher's Assistant) – An undergraduate or grad student who helps in some manner with a specific course. In some cases, a TA will teach a class, assist a professor, grade assignments, or conduct office hours.

Undergraduate – A student in the process of studying for his or her bachelor's degree.

About the Author

Well kids, all good things must come to an end, and CMC was indeed the best of things. It's been my pleasure to tell everyone how ridiculously amazing life at CMC is one last time before I graduate. I came over to the left coast four years ago not quite sure what to expect. I had been rejected from the school I had my heart set on, and I decided to take a risk and head to this CMC place, more because I wanted to be in California than because I knew anything about the school. Man, did I get lucky. It's been a great four years out here, and I'm not really willing to accept the fact that it's over. Still, I'm excited to head back east, start a new job, and settle in somewhere new. You, however, don't care what I'm doing next year; you're much more concerned with what you'll be doing next year. So, this is where I dispense a little personal advice about college as a reward to those of you who've read this far (and kudos to you for that, this is a long book).

Try not to stress about this process. It's amazing how intense and complex the college search has become, but there is shockingly little you can do at this point. Most of what colleges are evaluating you on you've already done. Sure, it helps if you get the best grades of your life first semester freshman year, and you can do a few things like interviewing with the admissions office, but mostly, your application is filled out.

Instead of worrying about whether what you've done is good enough to get you into the best tier of schools, think about this: college really is what you make of it. With a few exceptions, you can go to any school, and with the right mindset, you can get an excellent education, have a great social life, and accomplish whatever it is that you want to accomplish. College is just the where, not the how. Sure, there are some fringe benefits of going to a school like CMC: small classes, nice housing, good career services. But generally these are quality-of-life issues and you are adaptable and can live without them. So what am I trying to say? Good luck finding a school, I hope you find one you think fits you well and you get in. Should you not get in, however, keep in mind that getting into one college or another doesn't dictate anything about who you are, or what you can do.

There, it's a little touchy feely, but I've said it, and I believe it's true. I wish you a good search, come visit CMC, even if it's just to spend a fun overnight, and most of all: wish me good luck next year, as starting life in the real world can't be nearly as fun as starting college. Feel free to e-mail me at any time.

Hayes Humphries
hayeshumphries@collegeprowler.com

California Colleges

California dreamin'?
This book is a must have for you!

CALIFORNIA COLLEGES
7¼" X 10", 762 Pages Paperback
$29.95 Retail
1-59658-501-3

Stanford, UC Berkeley, Caltech—California is home
to some of America's greatest institutes of higher
learning. *California Colleges* gives the lowdown on 24
of the best, side by side, in one prodigious volume.

New England Colleges

Looking for peace in the Northeast?
Pick up this regional guide to New England!

NEW ENGLAND COLLEGES
7¼" X 10", 1015 Pages Paperback
$29.95 Retail
1-59658-504-8

New England is the birthplace of many prestigious universities, and with so many to choose from, picking the right school can be a tough decision. With inside information on over 34 competive Northeastern schools, *New England Colleges* provides the same high-quality information prospective students expect from College Prowler in one all-inclusive, easy-to-use reference.

Schools of the South

Headin' down south? This book will help you find your way to the perfect school!

SCHOOLS OF THE SOUTH
7¼" X 10", 773 Pages Paperback
$29.95 Retail
1-59658-503-X

Southern pride is always strong. Whether it's across town or across state, many Southern students are devoted to their home sweet home. *Schools of the South* offers an honest student perspective on 36 universities available south of the Mason-Dixon.

Untangling
the Ivy League

The ultimate book for everything Ivy!

UNTANGLING THE IVY LEAGUE
7¼" X 10", 567 Pages Paperback
$24.95 Retail
1-59658-500-5

Ivy League students, alumni, admissions officers, and other top insiders get together to tell it like it is. *Untangling the Ivy League* covers every aspect—from admissions and athletics to secret societies and urban legends—of the nation's eight oldest, wealthiest, and most competitive colleges and universities.

Tell Us What Life Is Really Like at Your School!

Have you ever wanted to let people know what your college is really like? Now's your chance to help millions of high school students choose the right college.

Let your voice be heard.

Check out *www.collegeprowler.com* for more info!

Need More Help?

Do you have more questions about this school?
Can't find a certain statistic? College Prowler is
here to help. We are the best source of college
information out there. We have a network
of thousands of students who can get the latest
information on any school to you ASAP.
E-mail us at info@collegeprowler.com with your
college-related questions.

E-Mail Us Your College-Related Questions!

Check out *www.collegeprowler.com* for more details.
1-800-290-2682

Write For Us!
Get published! Voice your opinion.

Writing a College Prowler guidebook is both fun and rewarding; our open-ended format allows your own creativity free reign. Our writers have been featured in national newspapers and have seen their names in bookstores across the country. Now is your chance to break into the publishing industry with one of the country's fastest-growing publishers!

Apply now at *www.collegeprowler.com*

Contact editor@collegeprowler.com or
call 1-800-290-2682 for more details.

Pros and Cons

Still can't figure out if this is the right school for you?
You've already read through this in-depth guide; why not
list the pros and cons? It will really help with narrowing down
your decision and determining whether or not
this school is right for you.

Pros	Cons
....	....
....	....
....	....
....	....
....	....
....	....
....	....
....	....
....	....
....	....
....	....
....	....
....	....

Pros and Cons

Still can't figure out if this is the right school for you? You've already read through this in-depth guide; why not t the pros and cons? It will really help with narrowing down your decision and determining whether or not this school is right for you.

Pros	Cons
....	....
....	....
....	....
....	....
....	....
....	....
....	....
....	....
....	....
....	....
....	....
....	....
....	....

Notes

Notes

....

....

....

....

....

....

....

....

....

....

....

....

....

....

Notes

....

....

....

....

....

....

....

....

....

....

....

....

....

Notes

Notes

....
....
....
....
....
....
....
....
....
....
....
....
....

Notes

....

....

....

....

....

....

....

....

....

....

....

....

....

....

Notes

....

....

....

....

....

....

....

....

....

....

....

....

....

Notes

....

....

....

....

....

....

....

....

....

....

....

....

....

....

Notes

Notes

....

....

....

....

....

....

....

....

....

....

....

....

....

....

Notes

....

....

....

....

....

....

....

....

....

....

....

....

....

Notes

....

....

....

....

....

....

....

....

....

....

....

....

....

....

Notes

....

....

....

....

....

....

....

....

....

....

....

....

....

....

Notes

....

....

....

....

....

....

....

....

....

....

....

....

....

....

Order now! • *collegeprowler.com* • 1.800.290.2682
Over 260 single-school guidebooks!

Albion College	Franklin & Marshall College	Ohio State University	University of Colorado
Alfred University	Furman University	Ohio University	University of Connecticut
Allegheny College	Geneva College	Ohio Wesleyan University	University of Delaware
American University	George Washington University	Old Dominion University	University of Denver
Amherst College	Georgetown University	Penn State University	University of Florida
Arizona State University	Georgia Tech	Pepperdine University	University of Georgia
Auburn University	Gettysburg College	Pitzer College	University of Illinois
Babson College	Gonzaga University	Pomona College	University of Iowa
Ball State University	Goucher College	Princeton University	University of Kansas
Bard College	Grinnell College	Providence College	University of Kentucky
Barnard College	Grove City College	Purdue University	University of Maine
Bates College	Guilford College	Reed College	University of Maryland
Baylor University	Gustavus Adolphus College	Rensselaer Polytechnic Institute	University of Massachusetts
Beloit College	Hamilton College	Rhode Island School of Design	University of Miami
Bentley College	Hampshire College	Rhodes College	University of Michigan
Binghamton University	Hampton University	Rice University	University of Minnesota
Birmingham Southern College	Hanover College	Rochester Institute of Technology	University of Mississippi
Boston College	Harvard University	Rollins College	University of Missouri
Boston University	Harvey Mudd College	Rutgers University	University of Nebraska
Bowdoin College	Haverford College	San Diego State University	University of New Hampshire
Brandeis University	Hofstra University	Santa Clara University	University of North Carolina
Brigham Young University	Hollins University	Sarah Lawrence College	University of Notre Dame
Brown University	Howard University	Scripps College	University of Oklahoma
Bryn Mawr College	Idaho State University	Seattle University	University of Oregon
Bucknell University	Illinois State University	Seton Hall University	University of Pennsylvania
Cal Poly	Illinois Wesleyan University	Simmons College	University of Pittsburgh
Cal Poly Pomona	Indiana University	Skidmore College	University of Puget Sound
Cal State Northridge	Iowa State University	Slippery Rock	University of Rhode Island
Cal State Sacramento	Ithaca College	Smith College	University of Richmond
Caltech	IUPUI	Southern Methodist University	University of Rochester
Carleton College	James Madison University	Southwestern University	University of San Diego
Carnegie Mellon University	Johns Hopkins University	Spelman College	University of San Francisco
Case Western Reserve	Juniata College	St. Joseph's University Philladelphia	University of South Carolina
Centenary College of Louisiana	Kansas State	St. John's University	University of South Dakota
Centre College	Kent State University	St. Louis University	University of South Florida
Claremont McKenna College	Kenyon College	St. Olaf College	University of Southern California
Clark Atlanta University	Lafayette College	Stanford University	University of Tennessee
Clark University	LaRoche College	Stetson University	University of Texas
Clemson University	Lawrence University	Stony Brook University	University of Utah
Colby College	Lehigh University	Susquehanna University	University of Vermont
Colgate University	Lewis & Clark College	Swarthmore College	University of Virginia
College of Charleston	Louisiana State University	Syracuse University	University of Washington
College of the Holy Cross	Loyola College in Maryland	Temple University	University of Wisconsin
College of William & Mary	Loyola Marymount University	Tennessee State University	UNLV
College of Wooster	Loyola University Chicago	Texas A & M University	Ursinus College
Colorado College	Loyola University New Orleans	Texas Christian University	Valparaiso University
Columbia University	Macalester College	Towson University	Vanderbilt University
Connecticut College	Marlboro College	Trinity College Connecticut	Vassar College
Cornell University	Marquette University	Trinity University Texas	Villanova University
Creighton University	McGill University	Truman State	Virginia Tech
CUNY Hunters College	Miami University of Ohio	Tufts University	Wake Forest University
Dartmouth College	Michigan State University	Tulane University	Warren Wilson College
Davidson College	Middle Tennessee State	UC Berkeley	Washington and Lee University
Denison University	Middlebury College	UC Davis	Washington University in St. Louis
DePauw University	Millsaps College	UC Irvine	Wellesley College
Dickinson College	MIT	UC Riverside	Wesleyan University
Drexel University	Montana State University	UC San Diego	West Point
Duke University	Mount Holyoke College	UC Santa Barbara	West Virginia University
Duquesne University	Muhlenberg College	UC Santa Cruz	Wheaton College IL
Earlham College	New York University	UCLA	Wheaton College MA
East Carolina University	North Carolina State	Union College	Whitman College
Elon University	Northeastern University	University at Albany	Wilkes University
Emerson College	Northern Arizona University	University at Buffalo	Williams College
Emory University	Northern Illinois University	University of Alabama	Xavier University
FIT	Northwestern University	University of Arizona	Yale University
Florida State University	Oberlin College	University of Central Florida	
Fordham University	Occidental College	University of Chicago	